7⁹⁵

Toller, Jane

Feb 25'74

English country
furniture

 51850

DATE			

© THE BAKER & TAYLOR CO.

English Country Furniture

English
Country
Furniture

JANE TOLLER

South Brunswick and New York:
A. S. Barnes and Company

Copyright © Jane Toller 1973

First American Edition published 1973 by A. S. Barnes & Co. Inc.
Cranbury, New Jersey 08512.

Library of Congress Catalogue Card Number: 73-46

ISBN: 0-498-01366-9

Printed in Great Britain

Contents

List of Illustrations

Introduction

This book is meant primarily to be a guide book for those interested in country furniture and who wish to have a general knowledge of all types of country-made pieces. It is not in any sense a text book, because I have tried, as much as is possible, not to become too technical in my descriptions, but just to give plain, easily understood information, with some historical details. Except for filling-in the background, I have confined myself to the period 1690 to 1840. Before 1690 the history of antique furniture is often complex, and much has already been written by various authorities on the subject. After 1840, the furniture, being machine-made to certain patterns, lost the appeal of the earlier and more original hand-made furniture.

Following the introduction of cabinet-makers to England in the Walnut Period and, later, the discovery of mahogany, the historians of eighteenth-century furniture have concentrated chiefly on fine cabinet-made pieces, country furniture not having been considered of sufficient account. The fascinating history of country furniture made by country craftsmen of country woods for country houses has, therefore, been sadly neglected.

I have tried in a concise way to remedy this, but it is not easy to give hard and fast rules to the newcomer to go by. No country-furniture maker went 'by the book', but by the needs of his customers, using the wood that was at hand. If Mrs

Smith wanted a table of unusual proportions he made her one. If Mr Brown wanted a chair of unusual size he had his wish. These pieces of furniture were unique, and not to be found in any fashionable cabinet-maker's drawing-book. In vain are the reference books searched for prototypes: there are no prototypes. The pieces were made for one special purpose, or one special person.

We once had a chair with a very curiously shaped back. It had been made for a hunchback in the eighteenth century when, alas, a hunchback was not an uncommon sight. Another, even more curious piece, resembled a broom in shape. The handle was nicely turned in stout mahogany and the 'broom' part, instead of holding bristles, was well padded and covered with red velvet. It turned out to be an implement to assist females to mount to the upper decks of coaches! As the lady was mounting, the upholstered part was placed just beneath her seat and she was given a gentle push. Perhaps a soft-headed broom may have been used in the first place, and from this common-place object the 'Ladies Assister' was evolved.

One of the many fascinations of collecting country furniture is the chance of finding something really out of the ordinary, another, that of possessing an article that will not be found anywhere else.

CHAPTER ONE

How Country Furniture Began

Country furniture appears to have a fascination equally strong both for the collector and the tyro, and there seems to be no particular reason why this should be so. It may be its originality, for no two pieces are really alike; or its naïvety, which is an endearing feature; or the woods from which it is made, for these in their diversity are a refreshing change from the more sophisticated mahogany and rosewood of 'town furniture'. There are several types of oak from which a great deal of country furniture was made; then come elm, sycamore, ash, beech, birch, pine, chestnut, cedar, yew, walnut, apple, pear, cherry, plum and mulberry—followed by woods for smaller articles (or for inlaying), such as laburnam, holly, box, bog-oak, and myrtle.

In order to have a better understanding of the reasons for the shape and names of the furniture that has been handed down to us, we must go back to its very beginnings, though, apart from mentioning a little about these early pieces, I shall not go deeply into the history of furniture made before the middle of the seventeenth century. This would take up too much time and space, and many excellent books have already been written on the subject. It is also becoming exceedingly rare, and correspondingly expensive.

To understand the why and wherefore of country furniture at all, it is necessary to know something of how it was made. Apart from 'primitive' furniture, which I will deal with later on, no one piece of furniture was made by one man alone. It took three or four craftsmen to complete the job. There was the Sawyer who cut the wood into sections, the Turner who turned the arms, legs and spindles on his lathe, the Carver who decorated the panels and friezes with his carving, and the Joiner—most important of all, who expertly joined all these various pieces together with wooden pegs, or stout hand-wrought iron nails made by the Blacksmith, who not only made nails, but the hinges, handles, bolts and lock-plates that were also needed.

Secondly, we must look at the kind of furniture that was used by our ancestors in the middle ages. The DINING TABLE (mostly made of oak) would have been considered the most important. This was made simply of narrow boards joined together and placed on trestles, and referred to as the 'board'. At first these boards were narrow, and people sat only on one side of them, keeping their backs against the wall for comfort as well as safety. They were served from the front of the table, and we can see good illustrations of this from early paintings of the Last Supper. Because the Gothic-revival Victorians had only seen these tables in use in the refectories of religious houses, they became known—romantically—as 'refectory' tables, and have been called so ever since, though many such tables were made for other secular purposes quite unconnected with eating.

A SERVING-TABLE was also found necessary, so a trestle and

board were set up against a side wall, and simply called a
'side-board'—a word still in use today. Later the boards were
fixed to legs, and became permanent pieces of furniture in
both cases.

BENCHES and STOOLS were used to sit to table on. A master
chair, in an important household, might have been made for
the use of the head of the house, and he might have allowed a
lower one to be provided for his wife, but the rest of the
household and also his guests sat on the benches and stools.
How hard customs die! Even today the modern set of dining
chairs consists of six 'single' chairs and two 'arms'—the latter
being intended for the host and hostess.

Another necessary piece of furniture was the CHEST for the
storage of clothes and linen. The earliest attempt at making
such a receptacle was to chop a tree down, and cut out a
suitably sized section, lay it on its side and hack off the top
side. The tree was then hollowed out until it was almost a
shell, the top part put back again with leather or iron hinges,
and it was then named, quite naturally, a 'trunk'. (And a
trunk is what we still call a large piece of luggage for the
carrying of clothes, though now it is possibly made of fibre
glass.) It was soon found however that the close proximity to
stone or earthen floors of these trunks was not good for clothes,
so a chest was made of six planks—top and bottom, front and
back, and the sides, which were made about a foot longer to
act as legs. Large quantities of plain and panelled chests were
made in the sixteenth and seventeenth centuries, which still
survive today, and they are just as popular as ever they were.

The other necessary piece of furniture we should mention
was the BED, made of four simple wooden posts holding the
tester from which the curtains hung. Very early beds were so
constructed that it was possible to accommodate a truckle bed
beneath them. It is interesting to know that the first important
cradles were made like miniature four-post beds on rockers.

It was not until the late seventeenth century, when beautiful lacquer and walnut cabinets were imported into this country from Holland, that cabinet-makers first made their appearance. These were Dutchmen who came over with the entourage of William of Orange. By a happy coincidence however, some little time before, we had given shelter to religious refugees from the continent, who had been cabinet-makers in their own country but came to England to work as joiners. It is believed that these men eventually taught their trade to the English furniture makers, which the latter quickly grasped and improved on, until in a comparatively short time they were acknowledged to be the best cabinet-makers in Europe.

Oak furniture gave place to inlaid walnut furniture towards the end of the seventeenth century, but our supplies of this latter wood, never very large, ran out, and for a short time we imported it from France (for the French walnut had the same curly grain). A disease in their trees stopped the importation, and in the early eighteenth century we brought mahogany from the West Indies and black walnut from Virginia. Both these woods, so very similar in appearance, altered the entire look of furniture, for they both possessed a straight grain which was no good for veneering—so furniture was made from the solid wood and ornamented by fine carving.

Everybody in the fashionable world now wanted mahogany furniture and London soon became the mecca of the cabinet-maker, and many men who later became famous established their businesses there. Thomas Chippendale (1718-79) was one of the pioneers, leaving the Yorkshire firm to which he had been apprenticed and setting up in London for himself. But a great many country cabinet-makers were content to stay where they were, and together with the carpenters engaged on large estates were responsible for making the country furniture we are all familiar with today.

By now chairs were considered a necessity, and not the luxury they had been in earlier times, so the trade of chair-maker now came to the fore. The country chair-makers however did not follow the London fashions slavishly but were happy to produce designs of their own, according to what part of the country they lived in, and influenced probably by tradition. So we get Lancashire spindle-backs, Yorkshire and Lincolnshire ladder-backs, Essex chairs with scooped out seats, and Buckinghamshire Windsors. Even when a more sophisticated type of chair was called for, the country chair-maker had his own idea of what it should look like. So we get a wonderful variety of country Chippendales, Hepplewhites and Sheratons in a diversity of country woods, mostly all with wooden seats. Wooden seats are not as uncomfortable as they sound though, and it must be remembered that up to the early nineteenth century when clothes became less voluminous, people wore their own padding in the form of many petticoats for the women, and full-skirted coats for the men.

The work of the country cabinet-maker came to an end in the middle of the nineteenth century when, alas, owing to the introduction of machine-made furniture, he had fallen on evil days. He was almost completely put out of work, having to eke out an existence by mending the squire's broken down furniture and making, whenever they were needed, 'coffins in the newest style', for coffin-making had always been the work of the cabinet-maker. Even Chippendale was a 'funeral furnisher'.

PRIMITIVE FURNITURE

This comparatively small section of country furniture is very difficult to date. Almost certainly it was made by the farmer with the aid of the local turner, and belongs equally to the seventeenth, eighteenth or early nineteenth centuries or, for that matter, to any period before that. It is both attractive and durable, and very suitable for furnishing early country cottages. All types of this furniture were made with three legs only, as can be seen from Plate 1. This was done purposely, for it must be remembered that the rooms for which it was intended had floors of uneven bricks, stone flags, stamped-down earth, or small cobbles, and three-legged furniture will balance easily on an uneven floor—a milking stool in a cowshed for instance.

The tops of the tables, and the seats of the chairs, stools, and benches, were cut straight from the trees that grew nearest to hand. The earliest ones were very thick and heavy, and one can see that the bark has been roughly hacked away from the underside. The usual woods employed were oak, elm, chestnut or walnut, the most favoured being that which contained the 'burr' or knotty part of the wood—for this attains a very high polish and has an interesting appearance. But whatever wood the seats and table tops were made of, the legs were nearly always of rounded ash, slightly thicker than broom handles, the reason being that ash is a hard wood and will stand up to a lot of weight.

There were two simple methods of making the TABLES:

1 Having cut the top to the desired size, three holes were bored right through the wood, into which the legs were pushed until the tops emerged an inch or so from the other side. These ends were split open, and wedges inserted and hammered in—they were then shaved away level with the table top.

2 A less primitive way, and one usually employed where the tops were of finer wood, was to fix a thick block of wood to the underside of the table with sturdy iron nails, and glue the legs firmly (or wedge from the sides) into deep holes made previously in the block.

Whichever method was used it was then a comparatively

Plate 1 (*above*) Primitive (probably home-made) three-legged stool, table and chair. Plate 2 (*below*) Small seventeenth-century oak refectory table with chamfered legs, and two oak benches. Originally in Ladye Place, Hurley, Berkshire

Plate 3 (*above*) Selection of country furniture, showing ash comb-back chair and oak cricket table with shelf

Plate 4 (*left*) Small refectory-type table in scrubbed oak, oak Delft-plate rack, an eighteenth-century hoop-back chair in ash

easy task to remove the legs when they became worn down, and insert fresh ones in the same holes. The factor that the legs were *meant* to be renewable should be remembered when buying these primitive pieces. Should *one* leg look newer than the other two, it should not detract from the value of the piece. Sometimes *all three* legs look much newer than the top, although the ends seem well worn.

On close inspection traces of red or green paint may be found. It was the practice in Wales and parts of the West of England to paint the legs in order to preserve the wood. If the table were to be used out of doors—outside a pub for instance—the whole of the table would be painted. From long experience I have found the red painted ones come from Wales, and those painted green from the West of England. Since this primitive furniture has now been collected for a long time, the paint will have been stripped from the legs by various purchasers, the whole table polished and, after long years of use, will now have attained a rich patina.

The legs of BENCHES were also wedged—but were always made of the same wood as the top—and not round but square, often strengthened by stretchers placed near the bottom of the legs at each end. They were used to sit to table on (Plate 2).

The shapes of CHAIRS vary. Some have waist-high spindle-backs, some shoulder high, occasionally one finds three-tiered backs on 'barbers' chairs. The top rails were always of the same wood as the seats, though the legs and spindles were frequently of ash. As there are more 'arms' to be found than 'singles', it is possible that they were used as fireside seats. A glance at Plate 3 will give a good idea of both shape and construction. The most exceptional type of primitive chair I have seen had a seat and 'arm-and-back rail' of 4in thick burr walnut. The arms ended with rounds sufficiently large to take a quarter tankard. The spindles and legs were of ash. It was indeed a master chair.

B

Three-legged STOOLS are made in a variety of heights, with different shaped tops—round, square, or oblong—and of an infinite variety of woods. For here the wood from smaller trees could be used, such as apple, pear, sycamore, etc. The tops were usually thick whatever the height. Some of the stools were high enough to sit to table on, others made shorter for children's use, and the shortest for milking-stools. The one illustrated in Plate 1 is of sycamore, with legs of willow.

The origin of these stools is of great antiquity. We see them pictured in ancient manuscripts—in tapestries and early paintings. They were often known as buffets or tuffets—Miss Muffet sat on one. And there is a very ancient conundrum it would not be out of place to mention here:

> Two-legs sat upon three-legs, with one leg on his knee,
> Up came four-legs, ran away with one leg,
> Up jumped two-legs, threw three-legs after four-legs
> And brought back one leg!

The answer is: one man sitting on a stool with a leg of mutton on his knee, up runs a dog and takes the mutton, up jumps the man, throws his stool after the dog—and brings back the mutton!

CHAPTER TWO

Tables of Various Kinds

DINING TABLES

Refectory-type Tables

The word 'refectory' means a dining room in a monastery, but no one could ever imagine that every refectory table came out of a monastery. It is just the fashionable name given nowadays to any longish oak antique table on four or more legs.

The earliest of these tables were very narrow because, as I have pointed out, people were intended to sit at one side only, with their backs to the wall, while the meal was served from the front. This was for two reasons: comfort and safety. The comfort of the diners was provided for by cushions placed against the wall for them to lean back on. (There were no chairs then in general use, only stools or benches.) As regards safety, no enemy could steal up behind the diners, while they were engaged in eating or drinking, and plunge a dagger into their backs—a very real danger in those early days. A relic of this necessity for safety occurs at modern banquets when the Loving Cup is passed round, for when the guest stands up to drink, the next guest rises to shield his back while he does so.

These narrow very early tables however are extremely rare and expensive and do not come under the category of country antiques. But it should always be remembered that very few of the later and more obtainable refectory tables are really wide enough for the modern idea of 'setting a table', which is why most women prefer a gate-leg table. There is always room in the centre of the latter for candelabra, cruets, flower arrangements etc, which is certainly not the case with a long narrow table.

Most of the refectory tables on the market today are of late seventeenth or early eighteenth century origin. These were made for the dining rooms of small manors, or large farmhouses. There are three general types:

1 Those with four or six balustered (or chamfered) legs, joined by stretchers all round the base a few inches from the ground. They had a frieze, probably carved, running round the top immediately under the board. This type is usually from two to four inches higher than average dining table height, which makes the question of chairs a problem. Stools or benches are really the most satisfactory answer.

2 Those with an X-shaped support at each end joined by a middle stretcher which went *through the middle* of the X, and was kept in place with large pegs on the outside. Ideally the 'boards' to these tables should be removable, as the whole idea of this piece was that it could be taken to pieces if necessary when more room space was wanted.

3 Those with a thickish baluster type of leg at each end (Plate 4) finishing on a wide foot to which the central stretcher was fixed. There was a matching piece of wood on the top of the legs to carry the board, which was nailed or pegged to it.

All these tables are getting hard to find, but the rustic kinds used in farmhouse kitchens are still to be had. These can range from five to seven or eight feet long. They had four stout legs, one at each corner, which were sometimes—not by any means always—joined by stretchers. A word of warning, as these were really working tables, not meant for sitting at, they had a deep frieze under the board itself, into which a drawer was placed at one, or both ends. (Sometimes one finds these drawers placed at the side, which means it was used against the wall.) This frieze is often too low to be able to sit to the table comfortably, especially if there is a bottom stretcher to contend with as well.

These kitchen tables were made of oak, ash, or elm, and though the legs were kept polished, the top was always scrubbed. Consequently, under the stain and polish with which it has probably more recently been treated, one can still feel and see the ridges made in the wood by the constant use of a stiff scrubbing brush. The boards themselves were not always made of one whole piece of wood. Nearly always they were joined down the middle, or composed of three or four planks. The joins invariably have opened due to age and use, and though they may be 'crumb-traps' it is not advisable to have them filled in, whether with 'stopper' or thin fillets of wood, for these never remain in place.

Another type of 'poor-man's refectory' is a larger edition of the pub table in stripped pine. These tables are considerably cheaper than those made of oak or elm, and can be stained and polished to be in keeping with oak dressers and country chairs. Plenty of deep wax polish is necessary in order to acquire a comparable patina, and it must not be forgotten that pine is a *soft* wood and marks easily.

Gate-leg Tables

It is my opinion that we in Britain took our ideas for these tables from those brought into this country by the Dutch who came to drain the east coast for us. Many of them stayed on and made England their home, and there is no doubt that Dutch ideas influenced very many forms of art over here. The shape of English gate-legs differs from the Dutch in the number of legs. The Dutch version had only four legs, but these were twice as thick as those on our gate-legs, and one at each end was split up the middle. These formed the gates to the table, and were pulled out to support the flaps.

The first kind of large gate-leg in our country had the two side 'gates' on pivots in the middle of the side stretchers. When the flaps were down one leg was closed against the two at one end, and the other leg joined those at the opposite end —making three in a row. After a short time the position of the gate was altered and put in 'off centre', as we know it at the present time. This position allowed for *two* gates at the same side, which was necessary on very large tables. Most gate-legs were supplied with one drawer, sometimes with two. It is a curious but true fact that one very rarely finds an early table with the original drawer—in fact quite often the drawer is missing altogether, and the empty space has been filled in

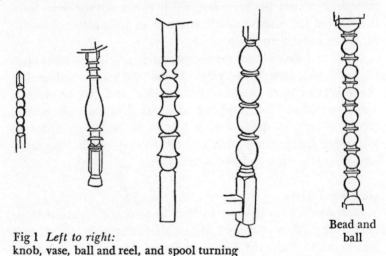

Bead and
ball

Fig 1 *Left to right:*
knob, vase, ball and reel, and spool turning

with a plain piece of wood.

The legs varied, but it is true to say that on the ordinary run of gate-leg tables of the late seventeenth century the legs were always 'turned'. There are various kinds of turning: baluster, barley-sugar twist, bead and ball, knob, ball and reel, and spool (Fig 1). The legs terminated either in small round knobs, or more rarely, 'Spanish' feet (which were rectangular ribbed feet widening at the base).

The tops of these medium to large-sized tables were usually made of four or five pieces of wood neatly joined together. If the middle section was broad, then one would expect to find it joined down the middle of its length. Each flap could be composed of two pieces with an additional 'tip' at the end. Smaller tables were made with fewer pieces. It depended of course on the size of the tree trunk from which the wood was cut.

Square topped tables are rare; for though they may have started life this way, the odds are that by the present time they have had the corners rounded or ovalled off. Most gate-leg tables are more or less round, and though occasionally a long narrow one makes its appearance, one gets the impression that it was a special order, probably made to fit a narrow room.

It is astonishing to remember that many a gate-leg table, doing yeoman service now, was made in the Cromwellian days by joiners and turners, before the days of cabinet-makers. They have never gone out of favour in all this time because they were so useful, but have been handed down in the family and therefore are still much in evidence today. I suppose they have been more reproduced than any other type of table and, when I say 'reproduced', I mean just that, for as far as I know I have never seen a 'faked' gate-leg table. Flaps have been replaced, as have the drawers and hinges; tips have been added to the ends of flaps from time to time as the original ones dropped off; the worn-out round feet at the bottom of the legs are often found to be replacements—but the main body of the table is the same as it was when it was made at least 250 years ago. In the eighteenth century the flaps were fixed in a different way to the middle section of the table. Instead of the old method of leaving an open space when the flaps were down, the new rule-joint covered the hinges. This, although perhaps looking neater, was made of very thin wood and therefore apt to break away over the old heavy iron hinges, and is never very satisfactory when mended. The rule-joint however gives an indication of the age of the piece.

Although too early for this book I should perhaps mention the first kind of gate-leg table. This was just intended to be used as a small occasional table. The middle section was supported at either end by a flat baluster leg, and the legs were joined together at the base by a wide centre stretcher. The legs and stretchers of the gates were made of plain unturned wood. The whole piece was lower than most tables, and very attractive. Occasionally the one baluster leg is replaced by two turned legs placed close together. This type of table, being rare and expensive, *has* been faked however.

Yeoman Tables

Another form of seventeenth-century gate-leg—usually of a smallish size—is known as a 'yeoman table', and was provided with one flap only. That there has never been another gate, is easily recognised by the fact that there is no 'notch' cut in the bottom stretcher for the leg of the gate to fit into when the flap is down. But there were sometimes *two* gates to hold the single flap, probably because it looked better that way. A long drawer was provided, often running the whole length of the middle section, and supplied with a knob, or 'drop' handle, at each end. These attractive and useful tables are much rarer than the usual type of gate-leg (Plate 5).

Drop-leaf Tables

As can well be imagined the idea of a table with flaps had come to stay but, in the eighteenth century, it had to be adapted to the general style of furniture that was now being made in Virginian walnut and mahogany. Instead of the turned legs of a previous period, plain rounded legs on club feet, or cabriole legs on spade, pad, or claw and ball feet, were all the rage. So the drop-leaf table was evolved. The top—square, oblong or oval—had two large flaps, working on rule-joints to hide the hinges. This was supported on four sturdy legs attached to a framework, two at opposite corners, and two forming the gates, which had wooden hinges. These were attached to the middle of the framework at the sides, and were either folded back against the ends, or pulled open to hold the flaps. This drop-leaf table with cabriole legs and claw and ball feet was very stylish, and became extremely popular; in some rare cases it was carried out beautifully in oak.

But though very suitable in the Manor House, such a table was not really big enough to accommodate the large families of the farmers; so a country edition was made in which the flaps were so big that they almost reached the ground. Because such flaps made the table very heavy it was supplied with six legs: one at each corner of the main section, and one at each side to pull out for the flaps to rest on. The legs were straight, either chamfered, or tapering slightly to end in a square 'shoe'. Occasionally these tables were made in pairs, and when they were joined together with the flaps open, could accommodate a large number of people.

These 'farmhouse' drop-leaves were purely functional, and not particularly pretty to look at either open or closed, so they can still be bought quite reasonably. When first made, the oak was of good quality and colour, but at a later date a poorer kind of oak was used of an uninteresting character, and for cheapness sake, only four legs were provided. This meant that the tables were not very stable, and country folk preferred the sturdy old gate-legs which, after all, if not in the height of fashion, went very well with their dressers.

Late Georgian and Regency dining tables were very rarely carried out in oak—their style was more suited to mahogany. So although one comes across them very occasionally, the following styles were not generally made: breakfast tables on tripod bases, or D-ended tables with spare leaves.

SIDE-TABLES

These were used for a variety of purposes and included card tables, dressing tables, and a late type of tea table. They were all evolved from the seventeenth-century side-table with turned legs joined by stretchers, and containing one drawer. This was followed by the Queen Anne walnut knee-hole table on cabriole legs, which had a shallow drawer in the centre flanked by two deeper ones. Both these tables were beautiful in form, and the latter did not lose a great deal by being made in oak, and nothing at all when fruitwood or yew-tree were used, in lieu of walnut. They were highly popular, and hundreds must have been made, for many beautiful ones remain with us to this day, not only to admire, but to acquire also. Perhaps there are not so many walnut ones left, and this is not surprising for the Walnut Age lasted a comparatively short time. But there are those made in oak, apple-wood, pear, cherry-wood, mulberry and yew to choose from.

The tables made in the early Georgian days were of a simpler form, with slightly cabriole legs ending in club or pad feet. One or more drawers were supplied to the table (Plates 6, 7, 8 and 9). Round about 1740 three-drawer tables appeared again, and the tables were more ornate. There were 'fretted' lattice-work triangles at each corner, joining the legs and body of the table, and the drawers were furnished with handsome cut-brass handles. The ornateness of the top part of the table was nicely balanced by the plainness of the legs—plain sturdy ones, which had the inner corners chamfered as a concession to lightness.

Later on in the Sheraton period the legs became much more slender, and were tapered. The tables were much lighter in construction. In the case of oak, lightness was further introduced by inlaying the top and round the drawers with a walnut or mahogany banding. Two, or even three, drawers were now quite common in the place of one long drawer.

With the Regency period there was comparatively little change, except that brass knobs, with decorated flat fronts, were now used; and the tables were taller and narrower to go with the rest of the furniture of that period, which was being made to furnish the high narrow Regency houses.

It is interesting to note how much the shape of everything in the Regency period differs from what came before or after it. The comfortable square rooms of earlier periods now became long and narrow and high. So did doors and windows, and the halls and staircases. Naturally the furniture had to change its shape too, and so did the ladies; for instead of wide hoops and plump curves above them, there were narrow clinging skirts with a waistline underneath the armpits, leaving hardly enough room for the rest of the figure. But these were all out of fashion again when Victoria ascended the throne, and women returned to hooped skirts which, as her reign went on, became wider and wider, so that doorways, staircases, and of course furniture, all had to change shape to accommodate the outrageous crinolines of the period.

But to return to Georgian side-tables made in the country, it is not difficult to date these, for there are many mahogany types of the Chippendale, Sheraton and Adam periods with which to compare them.

Tea Tables

The habit of tea-drinking, which spread through England like wildfire at the beginning of the eighteenth century gave us a new shape of table altogether, and made alterations necessary to existing tables. The tea equipage, whether of silver or porcelain, and the tea cups—at first with no handles— were set on a round silver tray. To take this tray comfortably the tripod table came into being.

These round tables had a tripod base springing from the main pillar. Many magnificently carved ones were made in mahogany in the Chippendale period with 'pie-crust' edges round the top, and carved knees on the legs, which ended in ball and claw feet. The tables were brought out specially for tea-drinking purposes, and were otherwise kept in a corner, so the top was made to tip up. Sometimes this top was on a revolving 'bird-cage' so that it could be turned round easily

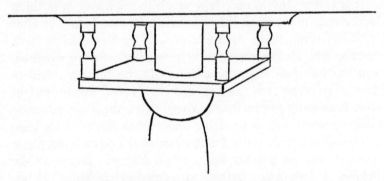

Fig 2 Eighteenth-century 'bird-cage' table top

(Fig 2). (The bird-cage could be wedged to prevent movement if necessary.) Then later, Sheraton tables relied on the beauty of the mahogany for decoration. These often had 'tray' tops (a rim round the edge of the table) and the legs and column or pillar were beautifully shaped, but not carved.

Round oak tables on a tripod base had been made in the seventeenth century for other purposes than tea—but these are extremely rare—I only remember seeing two. But now the new tripod tea table was made extensively in oak, and in country woods of all kinds. Charming fruitwood tables were made during this period, and some country cabinet-makers could not resist copying the amusing 'Manx' tables—the name given to the table where each of the three legs was shaped like a human one ending in a slippered foot.

The other form of tea table was like a CARD TABLE, ie an oblong table on four legs, usually placed against a wall. But instead of the top being covered with baize it was polished. This type of card table has two tops—the upper one is hinged and opens out, being supported by one of the four legs which pulls out for this purpose. Sometimes one finds two, or even three tops to these tables: one for cards, one marked out for backgammon, and the other plain and polished for tea. There is a contraption on the leg that pulls out to make it the right height to take each leaf as wanted. These tables are rarely met with made in oak. I think perhaps the country cabinet-maker found the hinges too complicated for him, because the country version of the same table, which has a polished top, has the flap permanently hanging down behind the table when not being used—much as that on a yeoman table might be.

Accompanying the tea-tables was a low small tripod table known as a KETTLE-TABLE or KETTLE-STAND. On this was placed the silver tea-kettle at a convenient height for the lady making and dispensing the tea to be able to pick it up easily. It must be remembered that at this time tea was an expensive commodity kept in beautiful tea-caddies in drawing rooms, and the hostess made the tea herself at table. These kettle-stands have been much copied in recent years for use at the side of chairs, and are usually known (quite wrongly) as coffee or wine tables. An *original* kettle-stand is almost impossible to find, and if one were fortunate enough to do so, the price would be extremely high. Most of those seen about and often, I am afraid, bought by the unsuspecting as genuine, are modern copies.

WINE-TABLES were made to stand wine glasses on. They were full height however, sometimes with a galleried edge and the tops were not made to tip up. This kind of table was also made higher but without the gallery and weighted in some way to take a candlestick or lamp. These are known as candle-stands or lamp-stands.

Cricket Tables

Round tables were of course not an innovation at this time in the country, for country folk had a three-legged form of their own, known as a cricket table (Plates 1 and 3). The query constantly arises as to how it got this name. Certainly not because of the three legs being similar to cricket stumps, for in early years only two stumps were used in the game. The answer is quite simple—if not as attractive. Small three-legged stools had been known for centuries in the north as 'crickets', therefore anything made in the same shape, but bigger all over, was known as a 'cricket table'. These vary quite considerably in form, beginning with the primitive type, referred to in Chapter 1. Those of later periods were made on an undercarriage like an ordinary table, to which three legs were fixed with wooden pegs. These legs either stood free; had stretchers joining the legs about half way down, on which sometimes a shelf was placed; or had one stretcher which joined two of the legs, and a second which joined that stretcher to the third leg.

A few had a small drawer in the undercarriage, and a very rare example had part of the top hinged so that it could be let down as a flap; two lopers supported this flap when up.

Coaching Tables

These tables were made to fold up, and were carried in the boot of the coach, and brought out when a meal was taken. They could be put up outside or inside the coach, depending on the width between the seats of the latter and the clemency of the weather. Although they exist, it is uncommon to find them in oak. Oak ones are much earlier in period than those made of mahogany and, though picturesque, present a more unwieldy shape for their purpose. They were in the form of very narrow low gate-legs, or like the one illustrated in Plate 10. It can be seen from the picture that the third leg is really a gate, which folds back against the other two, the top then folds neatly down, making it quite narrow for packing away.

Corner Tables

These were made for a particular card game—the name of which has been lost—for three people, and were therefore three-sided. When not in use the table was kept in a corner. After a comparatively short time the game went out of fashion, and that particular form of corner table was made no more. But another one took its place. This was made with four legs, one to pull out, and a flap which hung cornerways down in front. When the flap was up the table was square (Plate 9).

Pembroke Tables

These were small rectangular tables with two drop leaves and a drawer, the leaves when up being supported by wooden brackets that were hinged to the framework. They were said to have been an invention of the Earl of Pembroke in the eighteenth century. The earliest recorded one was made by Chippendale about 1771. They were also made by Sheraton and every other cabinet-maker of any consequence. Most Pembroke tables were fashioned in mahogany, but occasional ones are to be found in oak and yew-tree.

Work-tables

These pretty and useful little tables were practically always made in mahogany, or later in rosewood. Later still, a 'trumpet' shape, was made in walnut. Drawing-room or parlour furniture of the late eighteenth and nineteenth centuries was practically never made in oak.

The reason for this was a very feminine one. The drawing-room or parlour was always considered to be the lady's part of the house, and the ladies then, as now, liked to be in the fashion with their furnishings. The well-to-do farmer of this period was as wealthy as the squire at the Hall, and though he still might prefer oak for his dining-room, his wife saw no reason why her parlour furniture should not be in the prevailing fashion. So work-tables, card tables, tea tables, fire screens, secretaires, as well as chairs, sofas and stools *had* to be of mahogany. This applied to her bedroom furniture also. Heavy oak bedsteads were hopelessly out of date, so the new draped mahogany four-poster with its accompanying bed-steps and night-tables was installed. Oak was out of fashion for these rooms, and did not return as a fashionable wood until the Victorian Gothic revival.

LOW ANTIQUE TABLES

Before I end this chapter on tables, I think I should say that there is one type that is constantly asked for in antique shops, namely a 'low antique' tea or coffee table. Such things were, in fact, never made until the end of the nineteenth century, when two or three variations appeared, the 'Sutherland' table being the best known. This was a low type of table with a very narrow middle and two very long flaps, which was folded up and put away when not in use. It was

Plate 5 (*left*) Small
seventeenth-century
oak yeoman table and
rare child's high-chair
of the Lancashire
spindle-back type

Plate 6 (*below*) Fine
early eighteenth-century
oak side-table with
cabriole legs. The top
has an inlaid line of
walnut

Plate 7 (*above*) Early eighteenth-century oak side-table with pad feet. On the top is a Delft shaving bowl

Plate 8 (*right*) Eighteenth-century oak side-table with cabriole legs and pad feet. Carved pine mirror above

made of mahogany or ebonised wood, and was said to have been invented by the Duchess of Sutherland.

CUT-DOWN ANTIQUE TABLES

Between the wars, mahogany butler's trays were used as tea tables with the stands cut down to the appropriate size. Lacquered wood stands were also made to hold oblong papier-maché trays, the tray itself being covered by a piece of plate glass. Then, about ten years ago, came the craze for cutting down antique tripod tables. This was done by removing the top, and the block it was fixed to, then cutting off about four to six inches from the centre column and replacing the block and top. And yet there were a lot of satisfied customers confident that they had bought an untouched antique.

This operation was done on a massive scale, with no consideration given whatsoever to the type of table or wood that was used. Consequently a very great deal of irreparable damage was done to fine old tables of the Chippendale and Sheraton periods, and to fine woods such as walnut and yew-tree. In any case, even the humblest oak tripod table looks all out of proportion when treated in this way. The kind of table that is the least damaged is the 'bird cage' type of tripod. The 'bird cage' can be removed altogether from the axle on which it turns; the axle can then be cut flush with the block, and the table top fixed on to that. The column in this case goes untouched—but this still seems vandalism to me.

CHAPTER THREE

Regional and Other Chairs

WINDSOR CHAIRS

Windsor is the name given to the many varieties of 'stick-back' chairs. How they got the name is a mystery that has puzzled many collectors. It is a fact, however, that they have been known by this name since about 1740. Chairs of this type have been made all over the country since the eighteenth century, but perhaps the best known makers were those around High Wycombe in Buckinghamshire, and from this one would have expected to find the chairs called 'Wycombes'. I have never known of any *Windsor* chair-makers, but there were certainly at least two in Slough. One, who must have been chair-making in the mid-eighteenth century, labelled his chairs from 'Richard Hewitt Chairmaker at Slough in the Forest'. The one label I, personally, have seen is very hard, in places, to decipher, but mention of Windsor Forest occurs on it more than once. Slough at this time was little more than a few houses built beside a pond, in the parish of Upton, a small village 1½ miles north of Eton. It would not be surprising to find that parts of Windsor Forest were still lying

38

between the grounds of Eton College and the Bath Road at Upton. In any case there would be no lack of beechwood at Upton, as the famous Burnham Beeches are not far away.

As Richard Hewitt was only two miles from Windsor, and there was a good road thence through Datchet, he was more than likely to be one of the chair-makers who took advantage of the river to send their chairs to London from there. In the eighteenth and the first half of the nineteenth century, it was cheaper and more convenient to use the river instead of the roads for the carriage of goods. For instance the chair-makers of Wycombe sent their merchandise by carrier to Marlow to be loaded on to barges there. According to the trade directories of London there were two or three chair-makers who had warehouses or workshops on the riverside at Fulham and Chelsea, so landing the chairs direct to their destination would be no problem. Perhaps Richard Hewitt was the first to get his chairs into the London market, and that is how they got their name. The phrases 'The chairs have just arrived from Windsor' or 'When do you expect your next load of chairs from Windsor?' need not be repeated very often before they became 'Windsor chairs'. And it follows that any other chairs of the same shape whether they came from Windsor or not, would automatically become 'Windsors'.

The London chair-makers may have bought the component parts of the chairs to make up and stain for themselves, or even the chairs ready made, in order to save time and labour. And, lest any reader wonders why country chairs should be bought by London firms who were making much more superior ones for the town houses of the élite, it must be remembered that such chairs were highly popular, painted green or white, for use in both private and public gardens and parks. It is a fact that they were used at Ranelagh and Vauxhall gardens in the eighteenth century, and in the London parks up to the middle of the nineteenth century. They were also extensively used in London eating houses, **inns** and clubs.

Comb-backs

The earliest form of Windsor was that known as the comb-back from the resemblance of its top rail to a comb (Plate 3), though a hay-rake I think would be a better simile. Early chairs of this type had backs composed entirely of sticks which extended from the seats to the top rail. Some had a shaped splat in the middle of the back, which was either carved out in a design, or solid. Occasionally the better class of chair had a braced back. On these chairs the seat was extended for a few inches at the back immediately behind the splat. Into this two sticks were fitted, splayed out at an angle, and finally fixed into the top rail, thus giving added strength to the back.

Some of the earlier comb-backs had cabriole legs, and wide thick seats of ash or elm, hollowed out by an adze until they resembled a saddle. This form of seat, one of the most comfortable, was almost always used for any type of Windsor chair, especially the armchair.

Hoop-backs

The 'comb-back', which became very popular in America gave way in time to the one we are more familiar with, the hoop-back. This shape of back was one of the reasons why beech was such a popular wood for the making of Windsor chairs. The piece of thickish wood which formed the hoop had to be either boiled or steamed before it could be bent into shape; beech was flexible, and therefore an excellent wood for the purpose. Into holes in this hoop were thrust the sticks (or spindles) and splats, that had been fixed in the seats, and it is the splats in which we are most interested in the chair known as wheel-back.

Wheel-backs

Perhaps the original wheel-back chair had a back that really resembled a wheel, with spokes radiating from a flat hub in the middle. There could not have been many chairs made in this way, for out of the hundreds that have been through our hands I have only seen one, which was a beautiful single chair in yew-tree. The wheel-back chair, as we know it now, is one with a 'wheel' cut in the shaped splat that runs up the middle of the back. There were many other designs, such as the intertwined 'Gothic arch' (Plate 11), the 'Prince of Wales' feathers', the 'tulip', 'vase', 'cross' and 'draught'. This last-named was carved in relief, not pierced. There was also a very rare 'triple splat' type of back, which had one or more of the afore-mentioned designs carved out of each splat.

All these chairs were made in both 'singles' and 'arms', and although the hoops and arm-rails were of beech, the splat, spindles, stretchers and legs were often of a richer wood such as cherry, or some other fruitwood. Oak, not being flexible, was rarely used, which may come as a surprise to many.

Sets of six or more wheel-back chairs, are hard to find, and expensive to buy. A 'harlequin' set looks quite well, made of matching pairs—or even odd singles. There is one thing to look out for and avoid and that is 'café' chairs made between the wars. Some years ago there was a great changeover to coffee bars from the chintzy 'olde worlde' tea-rooms, a great many of which had been opened between 1920 and 1935 and were furnished with machine-made reproduction wheel-back chairs from Wycombe. The coffee bars wanted something more up-to-date, and the chairs were sold by auction, a dozen at a time, having had thirty or forty years of very hard wear, and much handling. I know for a fact that many of these chairs found their way into antique shops where most of them were sold as second-hand for about £5 a chair. But some got into the wrong hands, were polished up, and sold as

Georgian for three times that amount.

Careful examination will soon reveal that they are not antique. It is true that the legs are battered and the ends worn, through being scraped about on rough floors. But the seats are of uniform thickness, with very little shaping. The backs are identical, with 'wheel' designs, and there is not nearly enough wear and patina on the middle splat and top rail.

Yew-tree Chairs

Yew-tree Windsor chairs (Plate 26) are expensive because of their rarity, 'singles' are difficult to find. Most of them were made in the eighteenth and early nineteenth centuries, with either generous cabriole legs, or simply turned ones. The seats are nearly always of ash, which is capable of taking a high polish. They were stained a dark, reddish, brown.

There were two heights of backs to the arm-chairs. In the Midlands, where the chairs were made of a more yellowish yew-tree, traditionally from Sherwood Forest, the backs were higher than usual in order to accommodate the ornately shaped splats. There was far more, rather 'busy', turning on these chairs, especially to the arm supports and legs. They dated from 1820 to about 1880. Curiously enough I do not remember ever having seen a 'single' chair in the florid design, though there were any amount of armchairs still about in the Midlands in the 1940s. I think they must have been made to sell in pairs as fireside chairs. Before they became so rare many people collected sets of six or eight of these 'arms' to go round long refectory tables.

Yew was used for the hoops of yew-tree chairs. It was considered a flexible wood, because it had always been used for the making of bows in the days when bows and arrows were military weapons. Yew trees are supposed to have been specially reserved for this latter purpose, and certainly one

REGIONAL AND OTHER CHAIRS

finds very little early furniture made of yew-tree. Small 'treen' objects *were* made from the odds and ends of wood presumably left over from the bow-making.

GOTHIC-BACK chairs in yew-tree are very beautiful but rare. The top rail of these chairs was pointed not round, and made of two pieces of yew joined together at the apex. Instead of sticks they usually had three splats in each chair back: one in the middle and one at each side. These splats were carved like the tracery in a Gothic window and the legs were usually cabriole, both front and back, with a 'hoop' stretcher. There were modified editions of the Gothic chair, one being the more usual hoop-back with the middle splat being carved in the Gothic manner. Another modified type had no splat or sticks in the back at all, just entwined Gothic arches of the type illustrated in the Windsor chair (Plate 11).

Yew-tree chairs often have the maker's name stamped on them somewhere. Amos of Grantham is one that springs readily to my mind owing to one of those happy coincidences that sometimes occur to an antique collector. Many years ago we bought from a shop at Sidmouth in Devon, a set of four unusual yew-tree 'single' chairs. Each chair bore this mark, which we had not seen before, stamped on the back. A fortnight later we found a matching 'arm' in Burford in the Cotswolds, also marked 'Amos of Grantham'. Since then I have come across several chairs with this mark.

A warning! A few years ago someone was *adding arms and cabriole front legs to yew-tree 'single' chairs* from a yew tree cut down on some estate. But the fraud was apparent to anyone who knew Windsor chairs, for the seats were much too narrow for arm-chairs, and not even saddle-shaped.

Mendlesham Chairs

There was a unique variety of Windsor chair made by Daniel and Richard Day of Mendlesham, Suffolk, in the late eighteenth century. A mixture, one might say, of Windsor and Essex chairs (page 48). They were usually made of yew or fruitwood. The back of the seat was topped by two straight rails an inch or so apart, and joined at intervals by three small wooden balls. From these top rails came a nicely shaped splat, with carved-out designs. This was flanked by three sticks on either side. The splat and sticks ended in another pair of rails halfway down the back which were also joined by balls. The lower rail was not straight but curved downwards from the middle. The arms ended half-way round the seat, and had curved uprights to support them. The seat was saddle shaped, and the legs the same shape as Windsor chairs of the same date. These chairs, having been made by two men only during a short space of time, are extremely rare, and one would expect to have to pay a good price for them.

Dating Windsor Chairs

It is not difficult to date Windsor chairs, if one calls to mind the kind of dress worn during the period when they were made. Up to the beginning of the nineteenth century wide-skirted coats for men, and hooped skirts for women, were fashionable; so the seats of the armchairs were made wide enough to accommodate these clothes. The arms of the chairs finished half-way round the seats, and were cut away for the same reason.

The stretchers varied also. The front one of an eighteenth-century chair was bowed to make room for the hoop, and two small straight stretchers joined it to the back legs.

In the early nineteenth century, clothes for both sexes were skimpy in cut, consequently the seats of the chairs became narrower and the arms were brought right to the front, the supports being merely turned pieces of wood. The front stretchers ran from the front legs to the back, joined together by a straight stretcher across the middle.

After about 1850 the 'wheel-back' type of chair disappeared for a while, and its place was taken by chairs of a much more ordinary nature with a plain rail at the top and another at waist level. These were made in sets, and still called 'Windsors'. They were regarded as suitable chairs for the servants' hall or kitchen. They were well made of various woods, and look quite well in a cottage if nicely polished. But the hoop-backed Windsor chair had not lost its appeal. The Chiltern 'bodgers' never stopped making them by hand. The High Wycombe factories started making them also, and are doing so still, on conveyor belts in plain white wood.

LADDER-BACK CHAIRS

These chairs are almost as popular as Windsors. The idea of the 'ladder' would appear to have fascinated the chair-maker. It even fascinated Chippendale, and some very fine mahogany 'ladder-backs' were made in his workshops.

There are strong arguments in favour of the idea of these chairs having been introduced into the eastern counties of England by the Dutch who came there in the seventeenth century to show us how to drain what is now known as the Fen country.

Ladder-back chairs were frequently depicted in seventeenth-century Dutch paintings, at a time when the British had only just graduated from stools to the use of chairs, all with hard wooden seats, or at the best, leather ones. There had been English 'twig' chairs—what we would term 'wicker'—before this; these however were only made in 'singles'. When rushed chairs first appeared here, towards the end of the seventeenth century, the seats were referred to as 'matted', almost as though they had been made out of rush mats. Rush mats were known on the continent long before they became fashionable over here and there must have been plenty of rushes round the dykes in Holland, so perhaps it was the Dutch who evolved the process of weaving a rush seat *on to the chair itself*. From two inventories of seventeenth-century furniture in the Oxford University archives, we find interesting references which add strength to these arguments. Lord Teviot's Inventory (1694) mentions 'Eight Dutch matted chairs', and Bookseller Howell's Inventory (1697) refers to 'Seven Dutch Flagg Chairs'. There are many other references to 'matted' and 'flagg' chairs in the 1690s, according to Pauline Agius of the Furniture History Society who has made a survey of Oxford University and College furniture.

Another small point that might tie up with these theories is that though one could get chairs re-rushed easily and cheaply at High Wycombe towards the end of the 1930s, during the war re-rushing stopped altogether. This was due to the fact that all the rush used for the purpose had been imported from Holland, which was now in the hands of the Germans.

Probably everyone interested in antique country furniture knows what a ladder-back chair (Plate 12) looks like—the name itself is self-explanatory. The shape of these chairs, which were made of ash or elm, varies very little, but the shape of the 'rungs' or 'slats' of the chair *does* vary. Sometimes they were made with the bowed side uppermost, sometimes the other way on. Some of the 'rungs' were prettily 'scalloped', some were quite straight. The back 'stiles' and front legs were rounded like a broom handle, and ended in pad or ball feet. There were usually two stretchers at the sides, front, and back; or there might be just one, heavily-turned stretcher in front. The first type of ladder-back had cabriole legs in front and the 'stiles' at the back were extended above the last rung and ended in a rather elaborate finial, in accordance with the Dutch tradition.

The seats are, except in rare cases, rushed, and one ought to make sure, before buying, that the rush is in usable condition. Getting chairs re-rushed is an expensive and lengthy business, so that if any re-rushing is essential it can add considerably to the cost of the chair. Very often one finds that the legs of the armchairs have been cut down to make them more comfortable as fireside chairs. It is not too difficult a job to get these built up again if one wants them to be dining height. Like the Windsor chairs, late editions were made, this time for school chairs which now have been replaced. Sets have been made up from them, and as they have received a lot of hard wear an inexpert buyer can be led into thinking them antique. One quick way of getting a hint that they are not period chairs is to look at the colour, which is often a grubby grey. Another is that they are slightly smaller than average, and there are never any arm-chairs.

SPINDLE-BACKS

These chairs were made in the Lancashire and Cheshire districts and are very distinctive. They had the same shaped legs as the ladder-backs, but only three, or at the most four, rungs across the back. A top rung ran straight across the top, and had a shell-like carving in the middle. From this to the next rung a set of thin turned spindles ran. Below was another set of spindles which terminated in the third rung, which was usually placed about six inches above the seat. An armchair, being taller, had yet another set of spindles. Sometimes the top rung had 'ears' which jutted out at each end. The seats were rushed. These spindle-backs varied in colour from a golden brown to a very dark brown. They were made of ash or elm. Sometimes the spindles were flat instead of round. This certainly makes the chairs more comfortable, as the round turning is not very easy to lean back against, in fact a thin cushion is almost imperative for modern standards of comfort.

Essex Chairs

These rather pretty little chairs come, as their name suggests, from the eastern part of England. They bear a strong resemblance to the Mendlesham chairs (page 43), which is not surprising, as Essex is not far from Suffolk. They were a simple chair, made with hollowed out seats—comfortable to sit on without a cushion. In shape they were a simplified edition of the country-made Sheraton illustrated in Plate 13. There were two narrow rails across the chair at waist level, joined together in the middle by two or more small balls or, very rarely, a small piece of carving. Sometimes, narrow strips of wood joined the top to the waist-rail. The legs were straight, with straight stretchers. The chairs were made in fruitwood or elm. There are two drawbacks to them: the seats, when made all in one piece are liable to crack—they should be lined underneath with stout canvas to strengthen them; and, they are apt to be attractive to woodworm so should be regularly examined. But these disadvantages apart, they are very useful chairs to buy for a small cottage as they do not take up much room round a table, and look well anywhere in the house.

Nursing and Lace-makers' Chairs

These are two much shorter forms of both ladder- and spindle-back chairs. These chairs have not just simply been cut-down, but were deliberately made this height.

NURSING CHAIRS were provided with very low arms, so that the mother could rest her own arms comfortably upon them while nursing her baby. The front legs, which were turned and provided with pad feet, were four or five inches shorter than the normal ones, and the back legs were made short to match. Sometimes these chairs were provided with rockers—which one would expect.

LACE-MAKERS' CHAIRS have no arms and no rockers. They were made for women who were accustomed to holding the pillow on their laps, rather than on a stand. I believe they were used in the lace-making districts of Buckinghamshire, Bedfordshire and Huntingdonshire. In an old history of Buckinghamshire written in the early nineteenth century there is a picture of the interior of a Buckinghamshire cottage with a woman sitting on a low chair with her lace pillow on her lap. (There is also a very primitive baby-walker depicted.) In the days when four lace-makers sat round a candlestand (page 60) only low chairs could have been used.

COUNTRY CHIPPENDALES, HEPPLEWHITES AND SHERATONS

There is nothing much one can say about these chairs that they cannot say for themselves. They were country copies of the work of the above manufacturers, carried out in oak, elm, ash, birch and yew-tree. It is impossible here to go into the various characteristics of these three men, but any public library will have books on the subject.

Most of the country-made versions were made with hard seats, but not always. Country chair-makers had been getting more sophisticated, and their customers more particular, and by the end of the eighteenth century drop-in seats were more the rule than the exception for this particular kind of chair. What *is* astounding is the number that still have the original seats that were made for them. The old framework, horse-hair stuffing, even the webbing, are still in position.

When one removes the old worn outer-cover, there will probably be two more of different patterns underneath—it has evidently been too much work for the later upholsterers to remove several lots of old rusty tacks. Sometimes, since the first cover wore out, so many others have followed it that the wooden framework of the seat is riddled with tack holes, so much so that they might easily be mistaken for large-sized worm-holes. For this reason re-covering an old framework is a difficult job. One is always loath to cast away any original part of an antique chair, but sometimes it is absolutely essential to have a new seat made.

It should be remembered that each chair and its seat was numbered by the maker. Take great care therefore to see that the number on the seat corresponds with that on the chair, for they are *not* interchangeable. Being hand-made means slight differences will occur somewhere, and if a seat is forced into a chair it was not made for, trouble will follow. The joints will split open, and not only the joints, but very often the wood as well. The number can be seen scored in the wood in large Roman numerals at the back of the chair under the seat, and the corresponding number will be found on the framework of the seat itself. Should it be found necessary to have a new seat for any chair, be sure it is specially made to fit the chair for which it was intended, and given the same number. 'Rushed' drop-in seats were sometimes made, with corners of wood matching that of the chair.

The chair in Plate 13 at the left of the picture is an exceptionally fine country chair, beautifully proportioned, and a rich golden colour. It is early Chippendale in period and has, as will be noticed, a wooden seat. The next one to it, also a country Chippendale, has a drop-in seat, though it is more rustic in appearance as is the country Hepplewhite next to it. The Sheraton one at the end is cabinet-maker's work, with fine boxwood inlay in the top bar. This has a 'scooped' seat, and probably came from East Anglia, for most chairs from that part of England have this feature. All these chairs would be appropriate for use with gate-leg or drop-leaf tables.

Most chairs of the eighteenth and early nineteenth century, whether made in the town or the country, were produced originally in sets of twelve. The number may strike us as being rather large, but so were families at this time. It is extremely hard to find such a long set of chairs now. It is not easy to find a set of six, and one is grateful even for four. Since millions of these chairs must have been made, I am constantly being asked where they have all gone. One cannot altogether blame the export trade for this. Hundreds have gone abroad it is true, but not by any means all to America. A great many are bought by the Italians and Germans, who seem to like our country-made antiques. But hundreds of these chairs are still in this country—but not together in sets.

It was an unfortunate custom a couple of generations ago for the family to divide up the contents of the house on the death of their parents. Everything had to be shared out equally whether it made a mess of a set or not. So the twelve chairs got divided up between the family, and subdivided again about twenty-five years later. If every member of the family now lived at some distance from each other, it is easy to see how family treasures got disseminated all over the country, with not a hope of them ever being gathered together again.

Corner Chairs

Corner chairs (Plate 14) were called roundabout chairs in America, which seems a more appropriate name. There were many corner chairs most beautifully made in mahogany and walnut by the top cabinet-makers; but there were also several made of country woods such as oak, elm and fruitwood. Very occasionally they were made in pairs. It will be seen that they were fashioned with a leg in the middle of the front and back, and a leg at each side. From the back and side legs ran supports for the circular arm at the back. There was usually a splat, either carved out or plain, in the centre of each side. The chairs are more pleasant to look at than to sit on, if one attempts to do this in the ordinary way. But I am convinced that they were meant to be used *sideways*, so that whichever way one faces there will be a back to support one, and an arm to lean on.

This supposition is strengthened by the fact that there is a primitive corner chair pictured in Aronson's *Encyclopedia of Furniture* which came from Deerfield, Massachusetts, USA. This chair back was composed of two high 'ladders' joined at an angle, otherwise the shape was the same as any other corner chair. It is described as a 'courting' chair. The seat was only big enough for one person to sit on, so that quite obviously the man sat down sideways on it and took the girl on his knee, both would then have a back to support them.

Commode Chairs

So many really lovely walnut and mahogany commode chairs, with long shaped 'aprons' under the seats to disguise the pewter pots they held, have been 'converted' in late years, that there are now very few about in their original form. The 'works' of the chair have been removed, the aprons cut off and, with the original drop-in seats replaced, they now look like any ordinary antique arm-chair. But there were also commode chairs made in the country, of country woods, which people did not think were worth the cost of conversion, so we have not lost them altogether.

Occasionally, as well as the more sophisticated type, a really rough oak one turns up. Instead of a drop-in seat, there is a hinged one, which conceals the pine scrubbable one that contained the pewter pot. But pewter 'top-hats" fetch high prices now for use as *jardinières*, so it would be rare indeed to find one still in place.

Porter's Chairs

These large cumbersome oak chairs with sides and backs reaching to the floor were made with a shelf under the seat to hold the watchman's requisites; sometimes the front of the

Plate 9 (*above*) Oak side-table and rare oak corner table with flap, both eighteenth-century

Plate 10 (*right*) Unusually early oak folding coaching table with finely turned legs. Above it is a Chippendale period walnut-framed mirror containing the original glass

Plate 11 (*above*)
Eighteenth-century
Windsor chair beside an
oak and walnut long-case
clock, with gilt and
silvered face, by Richard
Lee of Great Marlow,
dated 1688; on the wall
a Yorkshire spoon rack

Plate 12 (*right*)
An unusual pair of
ladder-back chairs in
fruitwood flank an
eighteenth-century oak
chest-of-drawers with burr
walnut front. The mirror
has a walnut frame

chair beneath the seat is enclosed with a door. They were also made with a hooded top, in which case the framework was probably leather-covered. These chairs were intended for the use of porters and others who had to sit alone in the large draughty halls of public buildings and large houses. There was a smaller, more domestic type, made as a fireside chair for 'grandfathers', usually in oak or elm. These were made with winged sides, and sometimes there was a cupboard beneath the seat, or even a commode.

A smaller type still, also with winged sides, was supplied with a drawer under the seat, that pulled out sideways. As rockers were often added, this chair should surely be called a 'grandmother' chair.

Rocking-chairs

Several years ago there was an article in one of the leading dailies that stated categorically that rocking-chairs were an American invention, and they had only come into use in England since President Kennedy had started the fashion. This statement was so far from the fact that it was laughable. Rocking-chairs have been used in the British Isles ever since chairs replaced stools, and it must have been the early immigrant cabinet-makers from Britain who started the fashion in America.

Over here rocking-chairs were intended as nursing-chairs for the nurseries of the rich, and the parlours or kitchens of the middle and lower classes. They were never meant to be used as furnishings for the drawing-rooms of 'stately homes', and so one never sees them there. Nor does one see them on show in museums, for the simple reason that they are classed as domestic furniture. If, by some chance, one finds a cabinet-maker's style of rocking-chair, it did not start life as one; rockers have been added at some later time in its existence, and added rockers have to be well applied or the balance of

D

the chair is impaired.

The seventeenth-century rocking-chairs were made with the back legs slightly shorter than the front ones. A vertical slit about three inches long was made in the end of each foot, and into these slits thin rockers were fitted and pegged into place. This was done for easy replacement when the rockers wore out. The pegs were simply withdrawn and the worn rockers replaced and pegged in again. Rockers on early cradles were fixed in exactly the same way (page 162). When thicker rockers were invented, the legs were glued into holes in the upper side, as they are to this day.

A rocking-chair used as a nursing-chair either had very low arms or no arms at all. Rocking-chairs made as fireside chairs for the elderly had high backs and sides, and arms of a normal height. They were mainly the heavy oak or elm type described on page 55.

In the mid nineteenth century the contemporary caned mahogany nursing-chairs began to be made with rockers, and ornate bent-wood rocking-chairs, with footstools to match, came into fashion, closely followed by the new American rocker. These of course come under the heading of 'Victorian furniture', and therefore are out of the scope of this book.

Drunkard's Chair

This was the popular name given to a rare type of arm-chair. The ones I have seen have been made in oak, and were of the country-Chippendale era. The back worked on iron ratchets so that it could be lowered by degrees to an almost horizontal position. It was probably a copy of a mahogany padded chair intended for invalids, and was meant to be used in conjunction with a square stool (page 60) so that it could become almost a day-bed. It was for this reason I suppose that it was made very wide, so that pillows, shawls and rugs could be put in it to wrap round the patient.

CHAPTER FOUR

Stools, Settles and Benches

STOOLS

When country-made chairs came in during the eighteenth
century, stools, except for primitive purposes, went out of
production. There were plenty of sixteenth- and seventeenth-
century oak joint-stools about for use when wanted. So many
in fact that there are still a few untouched seventeenth-century examples about to this day. There were, however, stools
for special jobs that should be recorded here.

Potters' Stools

There are quite a number of these about for they were
thrown out not long ago from the old Coalport factory. These
are tall, four-legged stools with thick seats, either round or
square shaped. They are much more primitive, and not to be
confused with office stools.

Office Stools

Office stools had bigger seats containing hand-holes, and
stretchers which could be used as foot-rests. These stools were

made to go with the tall desks used from the end of the eighteenth century onwards, in merchants' offices and banks.

Coffin Stools

These stools (not to be confused with the earlier joint stool) were made in pairs by the undertaker who, it will be remembered, was also the cabinet-maker. They were used by him to hold the coffin both in the home and at the church. I have reason to believe that in the case of the well-to-do they were paid for by the relatives with the rest of the undertaker's expenses, and kept by them. (Doubtless the undertaker had a pair of his own for use at poorer funerals.) That they *were* made and used for this purpose is not supposition on my part, but a fact brought to my notice when about twenty-five years ago I bought a tall yew-tree stool with a hand-hole in the seat from the last two survivors of an old Marlow family who were getting rid of some surplus antiques. I had thought this stool was an unusually high joint-stool until the owner told me that there had been a pair of them specially made to hold the coffin of her great-great-grandfather, who was a man of some eminence. They had been taken out into the garden for some reason, and left there until one had succumbed to the ravages of the weather! I suppose in earlier days a couple of ordinary stools used about the house, or in the chancel of the church, would have been used for this purpose.

By Victorian days joint stools were things of the past —never seen in up-to-date genteel establishments. All the high stools they ever had in their houses were those which came in with the undertaker. These inevitably became known as 'coffin stools'. When these Victorians' children and grandchildren became interested in antiques and acquired a seventeenth-century oak stool, and showed it off with pride, parents and grand-parents alike held up their hands in horror exclaiming 'a *coffin* stool! I wouldn't have one in the house!'

And I have noticed that there is still an antipathy to joint stools in certain sections of the community for this very reason.

Commode Stools

Early commodes were known as 'close stools', probably because the pot was fixed in a stool enclosed all round with wood, and with a hinged seat. There are still seventeenth- and eighteenth-century oak stools of this nature (having been gutted) doing duty as fireside seats, log boxes, book or toy boxes and in some cases even as cellarettes or bottle boxes. I once came across a Chippendale period mahogany one in somebody's drawing-room doing duty as a piano-stool-cum-music holder.

The mahogany variety were usually incorporated in the bed steps used for climbing into four-post beds. These bed-steps, now beautifully covered with tooled leather, are used for quite other purposes in living rooms. I am convinced that most people imagine they are library steps.

Dressing Stools

These were usually made in walnut or mahogany, very often with cabriole legs, and covered with fine pieces of needlework, silk or velvet. Their equivalent in oak is hard to find, probably because the country wife, between her duties as wife, mother, and housekeeper, and all the several jobs these duties entailed, had little time to spend on her toilette. They were really luxuries for the rich.

Gout Stools

These were the prerogative of the rich. No poor man was supposed to suffer from gout, which was a rich man's disease. Indeed, if he needed to put his foot up, he could do so on any of the three-legged stools knocking about in his cottage.

All the gout stools I have seen have been the work of cabinet-makers, they were not country furniture.

Upholstered Square Stools

These made of oak are rare. They were used in conjunction with the 'adjustable back' chairs (see page 56) to put one's legs on, and thus make the chair into a sort of day bed. The stools therefore being chair-seat height are lower than most stools, and rather clumsy-looking, but very convenient to use as low tables.

Lace-maker's Candle-stand

Although this is *not* for sitting on, it looks like a tall three-legged stool with five holes in the seat. These stools are extremely rare—I have had the opportunity to find only one absolutely complete; it came from the north of Buckinghamshire, and is now in a museum in Europe. It is thought that Queen Catherine of Aragon, Henry VIII's first wife, first introduced pillow-lace making into England.

The middle hole was used to hold a *wax* candle. Round it were ranged four others, cut in at an angle to hold the 'flasks', which look like small round Victorian decanters filled with water with long thin necks which were tightly corked. These, being thrust into the angled holes, splayed outwards, casting their magnified light on to the lace pillows of the women sitting on low chairs round the stool, with their pillows on their knees. Thus four women could work by the light of one candle. The reason for this stringent economy was that wax candles were costly, being taxed, and tallow candles made of animal fats burned away far too quickly to be of any use, having to be constantly renewed. But four women could manage to afford one wax candle. Indeed it is astonishing how much more light comes through a water-magnified candle-stick.

SETTLES

These are good solid pieces of furniture, specially made for the kitchens and house places of farm houses, or for the bars of inns, and they could stand up to a lot of hard wear. This is evident, for there is hardly an old country pub which has not got one at least in use. Some even date back to the seventeenth century and are almost in their original condition. The feet are worn down it's true, but the carving is beautifully mellowed and polished with the rubbing of generations of rustic backs, and there is at least another couple of hundred years' wear in them.

'There is hardly a genuine antique in the country!' groan the Jeremiahs. Can it be that they don't know where to look? For in the small, and large, hostelries of England there is an enormous quantity of genuine untouched antiques in the shape of settles, seats, benches, tables, wainscot and Windsor chairs, cricket tables, long-case clocks, Act of Parliament clocks and many other things besides. But perhaps this early country stuff is not smart enough to be taken into consideration. It may be more useful than beautiful and perhaps not highly collectable but, nevertheless, it is antique, and apart from replaced hinges on chests and built up feet on settles, it is in untouched condition.

As this book is mainly about eighteenth and early nineteenth-century country furniture, I am not going into any details about settles of an earlier date that really belong to the Jacobean period. But eighteenth-century settles are satisfying things to look at and highly functional. Many of them serve the two purposes of seats and draught excluders.

A high backed settle, especially those built with wide curved backs, were meant to stand at right angles to the hearth; and many of these have stood there for years judging by the hollows worn on the stone-flagged floors in front of them by countless heavy boots. On these 'screen settles' the backs went right down to the floor. They were made of oak, ash or pine, and the backs were of wainscot panelling of the type known as 'tongue and groove', although this was usually used for the pine settles. The sides were continuous from top to bottom, with projecting ear pieces like the wing chairs of the period. The seats were thick, and often there were storage places below them, reached by turning back the hinged seats. Some, with more than normal high backs, had cupboards in them to hold sides of bacon. Some had cupboards that jutted out overhead like porches over a door. Some were made to stand outside a pub so that people could take their refreshment in the open air, and were provided with what have come to be known as 'pub' tables. If any reader wishes to know what 'weathered oak' furniture looks like, he can see it in perfection outside a country pub.

There was another kind of settle that was also very popular. Dating from about 1740 it was a long piece of furniture, always of oak, with a much lower back than the screen-settle, and a seat that was some four or five inches wider. This seated four or five adults comfortably. The back consisted of three or four 'fielded' panels. There were open arms at each end, and the front legs (one at each end and one in the middle) were cabriole in shape. The back legs were plain. The seats now will probably be of oak underneath the thick cushion, but in most cases this will have been a later addition. On examination, holes will be found at regular intervals in the framework of the seat. Through these holes ropes were laced along and across, in order to support the cushion, in exactly the same way as ropes were used to support the mattresses in early bedsteads. It is extremely rare to find these ropes in position. These settles are big pieces of furniture, only suitable for large rooms. One frequently sees them in the entrance halls, bars, and parlours of the larger hostelries once used as coaching inns. It is my opinion that they were specially made to act as emergency beds, should there be a sudden influx of guests at the inn.

It has often been remarked what a high polish this particular species of country furniture, ie that of inns, has achieved through the years. The answer is home-brewed ale. Beer is a splendid polish, and in case any of my readers would care to prove it I append the following recipe found in an early cookery book, which also gives 'Directions to Servants'.

TO GIVE A GLOSS TO FINE OAK-WAINSCOT

If greasy it must be washed with warm beer; then boil two quarts of strong beer, a bit of bees-wax as large as a walnut, and a large spoonful of sugar; wet it all over with a large brush, and when dry rub it till bright.

I am not sure what effect our modern beer would have on oak—perhaps it should be home brewed.

BENCHES

Unless one is prepared to pay into three figures for a Jacobean bench, one must be content with farmhouse or school benches. Farmhouse benches were made not so much for seats, but to stand things on, such as churns in dairies, or buckets outside scullery doors. They were made with very thick oak tops and wedged-in legs. There is also a more refined type of oak bench made with chamfered legs; probably these were used in schools. They are hard to find, but are well worth looking for, as they go very well with the farmhouse type of refectory table, and are really more suitable than chairs for this purpose (Plate 2).

Sometimes these benches have added 'aprons' for strength placed directly underneath the seats and attached to the legs at each end. I have always found this type of bench in an 'unstained' condition, always having been scrubbed. But they can quickly be stained to the desired colour with a good brand oil-stain. This can be obtained in three colours, light oak, dark oak, or walnut.

The objection is made that they are not comfortable in use, because of having no backs. But people do not lean back when eating and, afterwards, invariably lean forward on the table. Benches instead of chairs have two advantages: two benches can be purchased more cheaply than four chairs and more than two people can be seated on one bench—this is especially useful in the case of children.

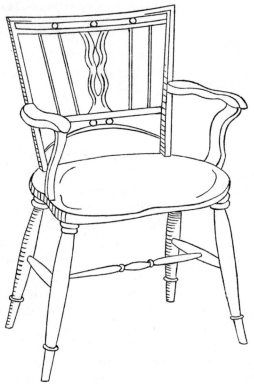

Fig 3 Mendlesham chair

CHAPTER FIVE

Dressers, Sideboards and Racks

DRESSERS

Dressers, contrary to popular opinion, are not necessarily Welsh, nor do they always have to be of oak. They were made all over Britain, and differ considerably in shape and colour, according to what part of the country they come from and the wood from which they are made. There are at least three different Welsh types, another kind from the North of England, and an entirely different variety from the district round Bridgwater in Somerset. Naturally, as there was more oak available than any other wood, most dressers are made of oak. But even oak can vary in grain and colour and that used was by no means always the very dark variety usually associated with Welsh furniture. There are many dressers made of elm, fruitwood and pine or deal. A few were made of walnut, and very rarely indeed, of yew-tree. If made of pine or deal, they were grained to resemble oak, or painted for use in a kitchen. 'Stripped' pine is quite a modern invention.

The fore-runner of the dresser was the primitive side-board, and it is interesting to see how each different type of dresser has been evolved from this. By the seventeenth century, the trestles of the side-board had been replaced by legs—four or six according to the length of the board. For the servitor's convenience, drawers were made, and fitted in the frieze under the table top. They were supplied with small wooden knobs or brass plates with a ring. There were three or four of these drawers, and they were usually decorated with different arrangements of moulding. These early oak sideboards, known as Jacobean sideboards, were quite narrow from back to front, and of a convenient height to serve food from. There are very few of them left.

This seventeenth-century sideboard was followed in the early eighteenth century by one similar in shape, but with cabriole legs in front, and plain ones at the back. It contained three drawers probably decorated with an inlay of walnut, and had brass 'drop' handles, or else handles with solid back-plates, for brass handles had now taken the place of wooden knobs. These Queen Anne sideboards are fine pieces of furniture, usually made of golden coloured, solid Virginian walnut or fruitwood, and are about five feet or more in length. They were used as serving-tables, and a plate-rack hung on the wall above them to hold the fashionable tinned earthenware plates (commonly known as English Delft) made at Lambeth, Liverpool, Bristol and Wincanton.

About 1720 the plate-racks went out of fashion. This was due to the introduction of mahogany and porcelain into the country. Mahogany was found to be an excellent wood for the making of elegant sideboards, and porcelain was valuable, easily breakable, and better displayed behind glass doors than on open shelves. So the hanging shelves were dispatched to the kitchen, and china cabinets took their place in the dining rooms of fashionable people.

Country people, however, were not so swayed by fashion as the more sophisticated town dwellers. The *liked* oak and country woods, which went better with the architecture of their houses. Sideboards were very useful pieces of furniture, so the country cabinet-maker used oak for making them. By now pewter had been in common use, for some time, but pewter is much heavier than earthenware, and much too weighty to put on hanging shelves. So, for safety's sake, the plate-rack had been fitted to the top of the sideboard, 'dressed' with a fine garnish of pewter, and the whole piece became known as a 'dresser'.

All this extra weight was obviously too much for four legs to carry, so two more legs were added to the front of the base, stretchers were added about six inches from the ground, on which a 'pot-board' was placed (see Plate 15). Sometimes the two middle legs ended on the pot-board, but more often they were the same length as the other four. By the middle of the eighteenth century, spice cabinets (page 109) had gone out with walnut furniture so a row of little spice drawers were often provided at the back of the dresser.

About 1760 the dressers became more stylish. Cock-beading (the raised edging applied to drawer-fronts) was being used, and the brass plates at the back of handles were carved out in designs instead of being solid. The front underneath the drawers was shaped, the legs well turned, and little drawers at either end, directly under the larger ones, were introduced. These were often dummies, however, used solely as decoration. The middle drawer was usually provided with a lock. Probably silver spoons and forks were kept in it.

Around 1790 the pot-board disappeared, except in the case of kitchen and farmhouse dressers, and the dresser was supported on four tapered legs in the Sheraton manner. The handles were larger, with moulded oval plates, identical with those on mahogany furniture of the same period. The racks were much lighter in appearance, the top shelf being reduced in height, and the top of the rack was supplied with a cornice similar to those on the bureau-bookcases of the time.

On the very big dressers used in farmhouse kitchens the pot-boards were often made of open laths, to allow the air to get all round the cheeses that were stood there to mature. This applies especially to pine dressers.

North of England Dressers

The rich manufacturers of eighteenth-century Yorkshire and Lancashire liked to be up-to-date and to have the new mahogany furniture in their dining-rooms, but since mahogany dressers were very rarely made (I have only seen one) the oak dressers which they found so useful were not abandoned in favour of sideboards, but made more elaborate to match the rest of the furniture. Mahogany inlay was used round the drawers. The escutcheons were often of ivory, and the best brass handles used. Cabriole legs were popular; and the rack contained cupboards on either side, very often with arched tops to the doors, which were also inlaid with mahogany, and supplied with locks and keys. The top of the rack was more important and ornate than those generally found on oak dressers.

Bridgwater Dressers

The most extraordinary dressers of all were those which came from the environs of Bridgwater. Primarily, I believe, they were only meant to be used to exhibit pewter, for the earliest examples have no drawers. For some reason the sides of these dressers were made all in one piece; in other words the rack could not be separated from the base. These sides were shaped, flaring out towards the middle, and again towards the bottom of the dresser (Plate 16).

With substantial sides like this, no legs were needed. Per-

haps it was a stronger way of making dressers, but though
they are interesting to look at, they are most unwieldy things
to move about, being exceedingly heavy, and difficult to get
through doors. They were made in elm as well as oak.

Cupboard Dressers (Welsh Dressers)

I should think it is correct to say that most dressers made
with cupboards are Welsh. They seem to have been more
popular there than in England; the English ones rarely had
racks, that is to say that they were used as sideboards only.
Most cupboard-dressers were made with bracket feet. Their
form was the usual one of three drawers with cupboards
underneath; the middle drawer was slightly smaller than the
other two. There was a cupboard beneath each end drawer,
and a plain panel in the middle, corresponding in width
to the drawer above it. The doors of the cupboards were
panelled, either plain or 'fielded' (ie moulded, grooved or
bevelled around a plain surface).

One of the Welsh varieties had an arrangement of three
drawers down the middle instead of a plain panel. Usually
these drawers were dummies, which meant that the whole
of the interior was one long cupboard, usually supplied with
one shelf. This variety was usually made in light oak, often
quite elaborate with 'canted' corners, and brass knobs on the
drawers and cupboards. Although it originated in the late
eighteenth century the shape was so popular that it continued
to be made right through to the end of the nineteenth century—probably even later. In dressers less than five feet wide
there were usually only two drawers, two cupboards, and no
middle panel. The small two-drawer variety made of dark
oak with a very heavy canopy, pictured in Plate 17 is undoubtedly Welsh. The way the shelves are fixed with pegs
to the sides of the rack is most unusual, as is the 'turned'
stick support to the canopy. It is a rare piece.

DRESSER RACKS

As each successive shelf on a dresser-rack widens, the sides of the rack were shaped accordingly. Sometimes they were most attractively carved out, others more severely shaped. The reason for this is a sensible one, small plates, etc, are more often needed than bigger ones, so they would be placed on the lowest shelf where they could be easily reached. The dinner plates were placed on the middle shelf and big dishes and chargers on the top shelf. Each shelf was provided with curved iron hooks, the ends blunted to avoid sharp points. Very big hooks for large jugs were on the top shelf, and smaller ones on the other two. Later on those curved hooks were replaced with ones shaped like the letter 'L' and when cups came into common use, the ordinary cup-hooks were provided. All the hooks were often removed at the beginning of this century when antiques began to be popular, and people were using the plate-rack merely to show off their Chinese plates.

The plate-rack should have a back of vertical boards: the broader the boards, the earlier the dresser. But it must be remembered that occasionally the original back may have rotted, owing to being placed against damp walls, in which case it will have been replaced with tongue-and-groove panelling. Dressers with the original back-boards can always command a higher price, and are more desirable, but a replacement is a necessity if the original boards have rotted, and this should not be considered too detrimental. Sometimes these boarded backs have been removed altogether. This happened very often in the thirties when open backs were considered desirable. If it is essential to replace them, it should be done with old wood, modern back-boards ruin the appearance of an antique dresser.

Sometimes it will be found that the backs have been

Plate 13 (*above*) Four typical country chairs. The two on the left are in the style of Chippendale; the other two are in Hepplewhite and Sheraton styles respectively. The first three are oak, the last fruitwood. Plate 14 (*below*) Three widely varying types of corner chair, all of the eighteenth century

Plate 15 (*left*) An early eighteenth-century oak dresser and rack, in original condition, with pot-board and wrought-iron hooks, furnished with a display of pewter and brass

Plate 16 (*below*) A selection of country furniture showing 'Bridgwater' dresser garnished with pewter, a fine oak joint stool, oak gate-leg table and Welsh stick-back chair

painted a dark bluey-green, like the interior of antique corner cupboards. This is almost impossible to remove, and in my opinion is better left alone. It makes a very good background for any plates, whether of delft, pewter, or blue and white Staffordshire. Otherwise it can be covered by staining with a 'dark oak' stain. One thing should be taken into consideration when talking about 'open racks'. If the room the dresser was intended for had panelled walls, a back to the plate-rack would be unnecessary. Examine the back carefully, and if no nail holes are apparent, no back has ever existed.

The shape of the top of the plate-rack gives us one of the best indications as to where the dresser was made. The Welsh dressers invariably had a canopied top (see Plate 17). Those with cupboards often had an extremely heavy canopy, and the sides of the rack were correspondingly heavy to support it. The tops of English plate-racks were light, and frequently quite plain with no suggestion of a canopy; for they had now quite forgotten about court cupboards, which were still great favourites with the Welsh.

Another characteristic of Welsh dressers was that the back-boards were placed horizontally across the backs, instead of being vertical. These boards were as a rule very wide and thick, and the idea has often crossed my mind that they would make splendid tops for refectory tables. Would this account I wonder, for their occasional disappearance?

DELFT PLATE-RACKS

These very rarely had backs. Such backs would have made them too heavy to hang on a wall with safety. A feature one often finds on these racks is a wooden bar placed midway across the front of each shelf. It was the custom in some countries to tilt the plates forward against them. I believe this type originally came from Holland (Plate 4).

E

NECESSARY REPLACEMENTS

We know that damp and dry rot can attack the back-boards of dressers, and that this has led to the renewing of the wood. Very often it will be found that the 'linings' or insides of dresser drawers have been renewed too. In the eighteenth century, such linings were often made of pine instead of oak. This was a custom handed down from the Age of Walnut since, when walnut veneer was first used on furniture in the seventeenth century it had been laid on oak. But this was soon found to be too strong for the purpose, as the veneer was inclined to 'jump' off. It was then remembered that the Dutch cabinet-makers used a soft wood for this purpose, so pine was substituted for oak to make the 'carcases' for walnut-veneered furniture and, naturally enough, for the rest of the interiors also. When solid mahogany came into fashion, oak linings were used once again, but the country cabinet-makers still continued to use pine.

Now pine, being a soft wood, is a favourite habitat of woodworm. These pests attacked the back and under parts of the drawers, for they prefer working in the dark, so their depredations went unnoticed for some time. If tools, or carving knives, or sharp-pronged forks had been kept in one of the drawers, they proved a menace also. Consequently the damaged linings had to be replaced and new oak, mistakenly, was often used for doing this. If replacements are necessary I always advise using sound old wood for the purpose. It is much more suitable, and far less obtrusive.

We must come to the vexed question of the replacement of handles. Those on drawers which get used a great deal are very rarely original, and I do not see how anyone can possibly expect them to be. Consider how often dresser drawers are used, whether in dining rooms or kitchens. At least three times a day the contents are taken out and, when the meal is over, replaced, which means the handles are used six times a day. A simple sum shows us that after 200 years' wear they will have been used more than 400,000 times.

Not many handles could stand up to so much tugging, the miracle is that there are any original handles left at all. What has happened in such cases is that the original single 'drop handle' fell off and eventually was lost, so it was replaced with the new type of handle that needed two holes. A hundred years later this handle had to be replaced again, and the now fashionable, long, early nineteenth-century oval one with an embossed back-plate was used. This again needed renewal in Victorian days when wooden knobs had come back into fashion. These knobs were large, and made with big wooden shanks which had to be glued into the drawers, so a hole at least three-quarters of an inch diameter had to be cut in the middle of the drawer. This certainly took in the original hole, but not the two on either side of it used for the long oval handles. Consider the dilemma of the dealer who has to find a suitable reproduction handle with a back-plate that will cover up all five holes, plus the indentations made in the surrounding wood by two differently shaped plates made in Georgian and Regency times.

Age, and constant pulling are not however always responsible for the introduction of reproduction handles on dressers and chests-of-drawers, etc. Very occasionally one finds a dresser with the small original wooden knobs still in place but, alas, not often. 'I like the dresser' says the purchaser, 'but my wife does not like the wooden knobs, she would prefer them to be replaced with brass handles.' How many young dealers can afford to face losing the sale of the dresser by refusing to perpetrate such a vandalism?

CHAPTER SIX

Chests, Chests-of-drawers, Chests-of-stands and Tall-boys

CHESTS

The names 'coffer' and 'chest' are now used indiscriminately for the same article of furniture, but originally a coffer was intended for the safe housing of valuables, gold and silver plate, etc, and presumably was made by the cofferer. There was also a smaller kind of coffer made for deeds, wills and other important papers inscribed on parchment.

Oak, though a very stout wood, is not proof against the ravages of rats and mice, who from time to time penetrated the coffers, and made nests of the parchments. So all such treasures were transferred to an 'ark'—an ark literally means 'a place of safety'. These arks were small coffers made with sharply steepened tops, like the roofs of houses, or like the actual house Noah lived in on his ark. Two holes were made

76

on either side of this ark, ropes were threaded through them, and the ark was then hoisted up to one of the stout beams in the roof and made fast there, well out of the way of nest-hunting rodents. The men who made these arks, or awks, were called ark-wrights, and many of our old cities contain an Arkwright Street where, centuries ago, all this work was carried out. Most chests and coffers are really too early to be included in this book but, as they actually overlapped into the eighteenth century, I have the excuse to write about them here.

As every woman knows, who possesses such a chest—and there are many genuine sixteenth and seventeenth century ones still about—there is nothing more irritating than having to move everything off the top of a chest in order to raise the lid to get something out. In these days we only use them for rugs or blankets, and therefore don't need to go to them very often. But originally they were the keeping places for everything, including clothes. The women must have complained for, towards the end of the seventeenth century, chests were made with a drawer fitted into the bottom. This drawer ran on 'bearers' fitted to the sides of the chest, corresponding grooves being made in the middle of the sides of the drawer, so that it was easily opened and shut. In some cases the chest was made in two parts: the base in which the drawer was placed; and the chest itself, which fitted on top of it (Plate 18).

This innovation must have been a great success for after a short time more and more drawers were called for, so that it was not long before the whole piece became a 'chest-of-drawers'. This piece of furniture has remained fashionable ever since, for no one has ever thought of anything better.

CHESTS-OF-DRAWERS

The early period chests-of-drawers were very bulky pieces,

for they had to contain the bulky garments of the period. The drawers were made in varying widths, usually a narrow one at the top for small articles, then a much deeper one, then another fairly narrow one, and at the bottom an extra deep one. They were decorated in the prevailing Jacobean fashion with heavy mouldings in geometric designs, very often with a different design on each drawer. The sides were pan-elled, and for easier transport the carcase was made in two parts which fitted together at the sides. Later in the period, with the introduction of smaller chests, this was found to be unnecessary, and they were made all in one piece again.

The framework of the carcase was of four posts, roughly about four inches square, into which the side and back panels were pegged. These posts extended at the bottom for about six inches to form the feet, which in the course of time became worn down by contact with damp stone flags. To cover up this untidy look, bracket feet were added at a later date—a fact which often puzzles newcomers to country furniture, who cannot reconcile the idea of Georgian bracket feet on a Jacob-ean piece.

A closer inspection will reveal the fact that the original feet are still there behind the 'new look' brackets; the latter can be removed, and the feet restored without too much cost or trouble.

These early chests-of-drawers were made of oak, elm, fruitwood or yew-tree, or a combination of these woods. As the moulded drawers were very heavy, strong handles were needed. Iron rings were sometimes used, but more often they were just elongated wooden knobs. The escutcheons were of iron or heavy brass. Later, brass handles were substituted, either round plates and rings or the heavy 'pear-drop' type, made with 'strap' fittings that went through a hole in the drawer, opened out, and then were fixed to the inside of the drawer with small nails.

William and Mary Period

In the William and Mary period the shape changed slightly. Chests-of-drawers were now taller and narrower, and much more elegant in appearance. The mouldings were done away with, except for a narrow framework round the edges of the drawers. The fronts were often entirely inlaid with another kind of wood: yew-tree, mulberry, laburnum, or walnut. Two small drawers now took the place of the one long top drawer, and the rest of the drawers were graduated. The feet were bun or onion in shape (Fig 4). Though walnut was now the fashionable wood, oak and fruitwood were still favourites in

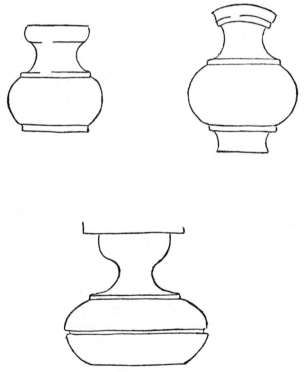

Fig 4   Bun or Onion feet

the country. A variety of brass pear-drop handles was used almost exclusively.

Queen Anne Period

Chests-of-drawers made in country workshops in the Queen Anne period were mostly of plain solid walnut with oak sides and tops. Where *veneered* walnut was used it was laid on a pine carcase, and the sides were often not veneered but stained, or even painted, to resemble walnut. This was quite a usual procedure. After years of patina and polish, it is often now very hard at a glance to tell the difference. There was a desperate shortage of English and French walnut suitable for veneering at this time, hence the economy. It is a great mistake to have these sides veneered now. The piece may not be worth so much as one with original walnut sides, but *if the original condition is altered* it will be worth considerably less for these reasons: it will not be an original antique and, secondly, an interesting piece that in itself is a record of the history of English furniture will be lost forever. Many chests-of-drawers were made of oak inlaid with other woods round the drawers and top, to give an added interest. The heavier ones were made in two parts as the Jacobean ones had been.

Although bun feet were still in fashion, bracket feet were now coming in, and indeed were often substituted for the worn out 'buns' of an earlier period. This can be detected by pulling out the bottom drawer, when round holes will be discovered in the base-board into which the original 'buns' had been inserted. One is lucky to find an early eighteenth-century chest-of-drawers with the original brass handles (Plate 12). The escutcheons however are more often than not original.

Later Chests-of-drawers

Country-made chests-of-drawers in each successive period

were made of almost every kind of wood including padouk—
a very heavy Eastern wood imported from China. They followed their mahogany prototypes in shape and style and were
embellished with inlays, or left almost startlingly plain. The
feet were of the bracket variety; brass handles of varying types
were used. Towards the end of the Georgian period, pine
bedroom furniture became fashionable. It was painted at first
in imitation of bamboo then, later, in grey or stone colours
with green or brown lines painted round the drawers and
edges of the top for decoration. The feet on these later chests-
of-drawers were elongated onion shape, the handles were
wooden knobs. When the fashion for pine died down, this
furniture was relegated to the servants' bedrooms, and there
it remained till the 1930s when it was brought back into
fashion again—repainted, and the wooden knobs replaced by
those of flowered china, and the 'onions' by bracket feet. These
chests-of-drawers are still with us, but now stripped down, and
waxed. I would like to say here that it is almost impossible to
get an antique country-made chest-of-drawers less than about
2ft 4in wide. One sees them sometimes in mahogany, but those
charming looking little pieces are really converted commodes,
which were originally made to resemble chests-of-drawers in
order to disguise their real use. The dummy drawers have
now been made into workable ones, and the top fixed. These
'dummy' pieces were rarely made in oak, country commodes
more often being made in the chair shape.

Linen-press Chests-of-drawers
   There *is* a small chest-of-drawers however which I should
mention here, which started life as a linen-press. There were
many different sizes of linen-press, from small ones for hand-
kerchiefs or napkins, which stood about on tables, to the
largest kind for bed-linen, which were fixed to the tops of
chests-of-drawers. The sheets, etc, having been pressed, were

stored in the drawers below while the next lot, fresh from the wash, occupied the press above. I should explain that in the days when these presses were made there were no mangles, no irons even, except goffering-irons, and so napkins, hander-chiefs, pillow-slips, sheets and table-cloths, had to be folded and placed in the presses, until they were pressed enough to put away in the drawers.

The kind of press that would be used for pillow-slips was in later years, with the coming of mangles, converted into a chest-of-drawers by simply cutting the 'press' off. The patina of age, or very probably slips of veneer, has now covered the marks of removal, but one can always recognise them for two reasons. Firstly, their smallness of size, ranging from about 2ft 4in to 2ft 6in. Secondly, the fact that they usually contain three narrow drawers at the top or, if they have been made in Norfolk or Suffolk, where the normal-sized top drawer would be is a very pretty arrangement of a small central cupboard (similar to those found in bureaux) flanked by two small drawers placed on top of each other. The cupboard door is usually decorated with an inlaid 'star'. These pieces in oak or walnut were intended for use in living rooms or bedrooms. They were beautifully made and would decorate any room, but they are rare and costly to purchase. Occasionally they are found with the press still intact on top.

Dust Preventers

Referring now to chests-of-drawers in general, the later and better-made ones contained a panel of wood between the drawers to act as a 'dust preventer'. Very often a fine powder is found on this caused by the constant friction of the bearers of the drawers being pulled in and out. This is often mistaken for woodworm. It is *not* woodworm but drawer dust which can easily be removed with a damp cloth.

CHESTS-ON-STANDS

Chests-on-stands were an early outcome of chests-of-drawers and considerably more elegant. The stand itself was like a low table with three or more drawers. There were varying shapes, of which the three more usual were:

1 A stand with a shaped apron under the drawers, supported on bun feet. This always looks as if it had lost its legs, but is quite normal.

2 A stand on turned legs ending in bun feet with two deep drawers at the sides and a smaller one in the middle. The legs are connected either with an X stretcher, or have continuous stretchers all round, sometimes slightly curved.

3 A stand, almost exactly like a three-drawer writing table on cabriole legs, with spade or pad feet—in mahogany this stand would have claw and ball feet.

Round the top of these stands was a piece of deep moulding, thus providing a recess to take the chest-of-drawers. This matched the base *in every particular*, a thing to remember when buying one of these good-looking and desirable pieces, for many 'marriages' can be found: either an honest one, because for some reason the original stand really needed replacing; or a dishonest one, to make an interesting and expensive piece out of the top half of a tall-boy for instance. A repaired or even replaced leg is admissable perhaps, but a made-up stand, even of old wood, is not really desirable. It should match the base, both inside as well as out. And, where handles are replacements, the marks made on the surrounding wood by the old handles should also match. I have seen evidence of knobs on the drawers of a top half, and none at all on the drawers in the stand. These pieces should always be bought from an experienced and trustworthy dealer; or well examined on view day if bought in a sale, especially if of veneered walnut, for veneer can conceal much unwanted evidence. Oak chests-on-stands are not so valuable, and therefore not so much worth the trouble and expense of faking.

The upper part of a chest-on-stand is in all respects like the chests-of-drawers of the same period, so needs no further description.

TALL-BOYS

These are simply chests-on-chests, which is what they are known as in America. What was said about single chests-of-drawers at the beginning of this chapter is applicable to double ones, with one or two minor differences. The main one is that the *bottom* half has a moulding round the top to take the upper part, while the upper half in many cases has three small drawers side by side at the top in place of the usual two. In early tall-boys the base is slightly wider than the top, and the moulding broader, to bridge the difference.

In the course of time many of the chests-on-chests have become separated from each other to do the duty of two low chests-of-drawers. Once, while checking the inventory of the furniture in a large mansion which had been occupied by the same family for 300 years, I came across the bottom part of what had obviously been a beautiful walnut tall-boy, listed as a chest-of-drawers, in one of the attic bedrooms. Apart from the fact that it had lost most of its original handles, and a few bits of veneer, it was not in bad condition. My suspicions were immediately aroused, so I went in search of the upper half, and found it in another range of attics some distance away, also listed as a chest-of-drawers. Quite thrilled with my find I went in search of the owner who, being a lover of antique walnut, was equally thrilled. The two halves were sent to a first-class cabinet-maker for repair, and returned some months later as an exceedingly fine walnut tall-boy of the Queen

Anne period which was immediately placed in the drawing-room. This piece had been relegated to the servants' rooms when walnut went out of fashion about 1720, and if the inventory had not been checked by someone with a knowledge of antiques it might never have been re-discovered, and a fine piece of furniture would have been lost forever.

It is not difficult to spot these 'divorces'. The lower half has now been fitted with another top, or, in the case of walnut, been veneered, and note—there is one long top drawer wider than is customary, and the whole effect is one of clumsiness. The upper half has now been fitted with feet, usually bracket, and of course will also have something not quite right about the top, which will look too heavy for the rest of it. Also if there are three drawers at the top where there would normally be only two, one's suspicions will be immediately aroused. It is as well therefore, when viewing the contents of a large house before the sale, to keep one's eyes open; it may not only be instructive, but advantageous. Occasionally in tall-boys there is an inbuilt secretaire drawer, but this occurs far more often in mahogany pieces than in country-made ones. The tall-boy in Plate 19 is an unusually fine pine one, surprisingly fitted with a secretaire drawer. It must once have formed part of a pine-panelled room, otherwise such a piece must surely have been made in mahogany. The Adam decoration on the top was probably repeated on the chimney-piece and door surrounds of the room.

CHAPTER SEVEN

Desks, Bureaux and Secretaires

There is a great scarcity of these much-needed pieces of furniture today but, before we get too impatient with the situation, let us remind ourselves that our ancestors were not accustomed to doing as much writing as we are. Therefore there was not the necessity for as many desks to be made, as there was for other pieces of more useful furniture.

The first kind of writing-desk was meant to be used on a table. It was about two feet wide and made with a sloping lid which hinged on to a narrow piece of wood at the top. Inside, at the back, were a range of pigeon-holes, with a row of small drawers underneath them, the rest was one big receptacle for papers. The 'scribe', for so I feel he should be called, sat or stood to this desk to work out his accounts, write his letters, and maybe even his diary. But every time he wished to get to the pigeon-holes and drawers, or to the rest of his papers, he had to raise the writing-lid to do so. This had to be remedied, consequently we find a later type of writing-desk where the

86

hinges were placed at *the bottom of the lid* so that it could be opened and lowered till it rested on the table; the pigeon-holes and small drawers were now readily accessible. A little later a drawer was made in the bottom of the desk and 'lopers' fitted at each side to pull out for the lid to rest on. ('Lopers' are the long sticks furnished with small brass knobs, found at the extreme sides of the base of a bureau beneath the lid.) From this table-desk two different types of writing-desk developed: desks on legs and bureaux.

DESKS ON LEGS

Writing-desks

The easiest way of making a piece of furniture out of a table-desk was to mount it on legs. These legs were attached to a frame-work into which the desk fitted. A few of these very early writing-desks on legs, dating from the seventeenth century, still exist *in their original form*. Others have been made more recently by supplying a base to the table-desk, made of old oak. These are really no use as writing-desks as most of them, being hinged at the top, are too inconvenient, but they are excellent pieces of furniture for a hall. The interior of the desk makes a splendid receptacle for gloves, scarves, dog-leashes, etc. A telephone will sit on the narrow part at the top, and if there is a drawer in the base, the telephone directories can be put in that. The price should be reasonable, as it cannot properly be described as a genuine antique.

This type of desk on straight legs went out of fashion as a piece of household furniture quite quickly, although a higher and wider type was used up to the end of the nineteenth century in merchants' offices, and the old-fashioned banks. And what is even more interesting, if not the originals, almost their exact counterparts are still being used in schools to this day. Round about 1720 larger oak desks were made to fit on 'table' bases, which had a drawer or drawers. These table bases had cabriole legs, with spade, pad or ball and claw feet. The result was a most attractive and useful piece of furniture. The interior of such a desk hardly needs describing, being the usual arrangement of pigeon-holes over small drawers. These pigeon-holes often had a little carved canopy at the top—and not just for decoration. Pull at one gently, it may turn out to be a very narrow drawer, suitable for hiding a few guineas or a £5 note in case of an emergency. When mahogany came in, this type of desk went out of fashion. One wonders why, but the fact remains that, of those available now, a very few are of walnut or fruitwood, the greatest number being of oak.

Special Desks

There were other, more specialised, kinds of desks, such as those for architects and artists; but as these were made by highly proficient cabinet-makers, in mahogany, they can hardly come into the category of country furniture. However, I once bought a really beautiful music desk made in oak, which I think ought to be described here. It was in the form of a tripod table with a square top. This top was double, and the upper half was hinged so that it could make, when raised, a desk for music. Under the table were two flat round candle-slides on pivots, that could be pulled out for use when necessary. It was a very well-made piece in a lovely golden coloured oak. Although it was one of the first pieces of furniture I bought for my shop in St Christopher's Place in 1934, it impressed itself so well on my memory that I can remember very well both the name of the man I bought it from, and the one to whom I sold it.

BUREAUX

It may have been just by chance that one day the desk was

Plate 17 (*right*) An interesting
small early eighteenth-century
oak Welsh dresser with
cupboards

Plate 18 (*below*) Early
eighteenth-century low oak chest
on bracket feet with drawers
in base. Original handles
and escutcheon

Plate 19 (*above*) Fine
stripped-pine tall-boy
with canted grooved
sides and bracket feet.
The fittings to the
secretaire drawer are
veneered with
satinwood

Plate 20 (*right*) William
and Mary oak bureau.
Note the way the desk
part overlaps the
chest-of-drawers on
which it stands—a
feature of these very
early bureaux

picked up off the table and plonked down on a chest-of-drawers. Or possibly the need for more drawer-room for papers
became urgent. In any case the desk has, so to speak, remained
on a chest-of-drawers ever since, and the whole piece became
a 'bureau'. An eighteenth-century dictionary gives the defini-
tion of the word 'bureau' as a 'chest-of-drawers', so it may
have been the fashionable name of that piece of furniture in
those days, whether or not it had a desk on top. When, towards
the end of the seventeenth century the bureau made its
appearance, the desk part was made slightly wider than the
base, and jutted out at each side. It was removable, merely
being fixed to the base with two pegs or screws. It is a rare
thing to find one of these early bureaux in good condition.

In the early eighteenth century the two parts of the piece,
although still separate entities were made the same size, the
join being covered at the front and sides by a piece of moulding. Very often another piece of moulding was fixed at the
bottom of the outside of the lid, so that when closed it could
be used as a book-rest, music-rack, or even an easel. The drawers and pigeon-holes were still there but the 'well' beneath
them was covered with a sliding lid, which gave greater writing space.

The next step was quite a big one—the sides of the bureau
were now made *all in one piece*, and the desk became an
integral part of the whole, so that no moulding round the
desk part was needed. The 'well' was now entirely done away
with, and at the top of the drawer section, were now two small
drawers. The lopers were still there, but very occasionally
they were replaced by extremely narrow drawers (semi-secret
receptacles) which could be pulled out to support the lid.

Towards the middle of the eighteenth century the desk
interior was altered. Instead of a range of pigeon-holes and
drawers all along the top, a small cupboard was placed in the
middle, which was an architectural item almost like a minia-

F

ture front door flanked by two columns. These columns, which looked quite solid, were in fact hollow inside, and could be pulled out and used as drawers. Pigeon-holes were ranged on either side, and underneath them the drawers went up in steps, sometimes in a semi-circle, which gave a very attractive effect. Small brass handles were placed on the drawers, and a lock and escutcheon on the cupboard door.

The woods used for the early bureaux were walnut and oak, afterwards other country woods were employed. There is no need to give a special description of the lower part of a bureau, for it was exactly similar in all respects to the chests-of-drawers of the period in which it was made (Plates 20-24).

Bureau-bookcases

When books became more common it was necessary to house them somewhere, but they were valuable things that had to be kept away from dust. So a bookcase with movable shelves, enclosed with solid doors, was fitted to the top of the bureau and the whole piece was called a 'bureau-bookcase'. Those made in lacquer by talented craftsmen are about the most handsome pieces of furniture ever invented, but as they could never conceivably come under the heading of country furniture, the reader must seek a detailed description elsewhere. Those made in walnut were equally splendid, often being made with a double-domed top and with bevelled mirror-glass door. This top was made flush with the drawer part below. Beneath the mirror doors were fixed two pull-out slides for candle-sticks to give light, when necessary, to those using the desk. When lit, the effect of the candles mirrored in the glass behind them must have been exceedingly attractive, and not only attractive, but an ingenious way of increasing the light in the room.

Oak bureau-bookcases were plainer—I have never seen one

with a double-domed top for instance—and the doors were of solid oak, relying for their interest on the grain and colour of the wood. Instead of glass, fielded panels with domed tops were inserted in the doors, often decorated with a line of walnut inlay following the shape of the panels. They had candle slides, and the insides of the cupboards were fitted with numerous lateral slips of wood into which the shelves could be slid in and out with ease, and placed at heights suitable to accommodate the different sized books. Alas, it is not very easy these days to obtain these useful and desirable pieces of furniture.

In later days the early walnut bureau-bookcases were spoiled by having the mirror-glass removed from the doors, and plain glass fitted in its place. But no one thought enough of the oak variety to bother to make this change, so fine specimens can still be found in their original condition. When mahogany took the place of walnut, glass doors, decorated with various shaped astragals, were used once more, and the bureau-book-case should have been renamed 'bureau-cabinet', for now the interior shelves were used to display fine porcelain.

Eton 'Burry'

Living in Eton as I do I cannot leave the subject of bureau-bookcases without describing the piece of furniture every old Etonian refers to as an Eton 'burry'. Unless one *does* know about these pieces of furniture, they can cause much speculation, because of their very narrow width which I do not think can ever be more than two foot six inches, although the height is much as usual. The 'burry' followed the usual pattern, drawers below and cupboards above; but the cupboard doors in many cases have carvings or even paintings on them, the work of successive owners. These pieces of furniture were made in the eighteenth century by the school carpenter to stand between the beds in the dormitory known as the Long

Chamber at Eton College and were for the use of the boys.
The latter not only used them for work, but must have spent
much leisure time in decorating them. I can only conjecture
that they were allowed to buy these burrys when they left the
College, otherwise such pieces could never have appeared on
the open market.

They are quite genuine, though rather rough, antiques;
but not highly valuable, except from an historical point of
view. It is interesting to note the corruption of the word
'bureau' to 'burry'.

THE SECRETAIRE

This was a chest-of-drawers made with a deep top drawer
which, when it had been pulled out about half-way, was
checked, and the front of the drawer could then be let down
on internal side hinges, to form part of the desk, the rest
of the desk being the bottom of the drawer, which contained
pigeon-holes, etc, at the back. These secretaires originated in
the first decade of the eighteenth century, but became more
popular with the introduction of mahogany, and were very
fashionable indeed round about 1770-90, when they were
introduced into various pieces of furniture such as tall-boys,
bookcases, and even sideboards.

The Secretaire-bookcase

This was the favourite form of secretaire—in fact its base
was the secretaire, on to which a bookcase that was not quite
as deep as the base was fitted, being set back about five or
six inches. The doors were fitted with plain glass divided by
astragals, and the whole top half was really intended as a
'display cabinet' more than a bookcase. When, in rare cases,
these pieces were made in oak, the doors were usually not
glazed, but made of solid oak like those of the bureau-book-

cases. Mahogany and rosewood secretaire-bookcases remained popular right up to Victorian days, but for some reason were not copied much in other woods by the country cabinet-maker.

KNEE-HOLE DESK

The earliest type of this desk was a small, essentially feminine, piece made in the early eighteenth century of walnut for the furnishing of a boudoir or drawing-room. I am quite sure these very desirable attractive pieces were never intended for serious writing. They are much too small even to accommodate *one* knee in the knee-hole and were especially so for a lady hedged round in the hooped skirts of the period. She was supposed to sit at it merely to dash off an invitation, or a not very serious *billet-doux*.

There were drawers down either side of the knee-hole. Halfway down the aperture was a small cupboard; for what purpose I cannot think, since it was not large enough to hold anything useful. Across the drawers and the knee-hole, immediately under the top, was one long drawer, sometimes fitted with compartments for toilette accessories. These desks are expensive, have been much copied, and were seldom made in oak. When an oak one was made, however, it was in a slightly larger and more useful size, well proportioned, and of a fine colour. They are *not* common, and whoever possesses one is indeed fortunate.

Later on, in the Georgian period, when *large* mahogany knee-hole and partners' desks were being made, a few oak editions appeared, made probably for the merchant or lawyer. This type of knee-hole rarely had a cupboard, instead there was a middle aperture which comfortably accommodated both knees, and ran from back to front. Strangely the price for this very useful piece of furniture, with its original brass handles and bracket feet, is much less than that of its Victorian counterpart in mahogany, most examples of which have now been 'prettied' up by having the original wooden knobs replaced with brass ones, and the tops inlaid with a tooled synthetic leather in red or green.

FALL-FLAP BUREAUX

These date back to the end of the seventeenth century, and were probably Dutch in origin. They were made in walnut, oak and fruitwood, and are very beautiful pieces of furniture. The base, slightly wider than the top, was a chest-of-drawers on bun feet, and a wide piece of moulding was set round the top to take the upper part, which was the writing-desk. The front of this was one large flap, hinged at the bottom, which let down to form a wide desk. Inside were pigeon-holes, and several small drawers set symmetrically round a small cupboard similar to that in a bureau. These in turn hid other, secret, drawers, hidden in a very cunning way.

Over the flap, immediately under the cornice, was a rounded piece of moulding, which was in fact the front of yet another drawer. As this had no handles, to the uninitiated it would appear to be part of the cornice, so could almost be called another secret drawer. The only disadvantage of these fall-flap bureaux, is the wideness of the flap from front to back which prevents the writer from reaching the pigeon-holes, etc, in comfort.

I once bought a very fine late seventeenth-century fall-flap bureau, and was informed by the owner that before going on her holidays she had put the greater part of her jewellery in the most secret of the secret drawers. On her return she found that the house had been ransacked by thieves, and almost everything of any value had been taken, but her jewellery was still intact in the secret drawer of her desk. A piece of this age, even in oak, can be very costly, but perhaps no more costly than having a wall safe installed.

SECRET DRAWERS

These occur so much more often in writing-desks and bureaux than in any other piece, that I feel this is the place to give hints as to where to look for them. Usually they are found when cleaning or renovating a piece—and this should stimulate the lazy to action.

I have mentioned the 'pillar' and 'canopy' drawers, but there is often another small drawer hidden at the back of one of the longer drawers under the pigeon-holes. Take out the drawers and measure them, checking them against the measurements of the *outside* of the desk, and if there is a discrepancy, then feel at the back of the aperture for a false drawer. There will possibly be no clue to help you, but if the drawer is next to the cupboard—then see if the *whole* of the cupboard will pull out, if it will, feel inside for a spring that will release the drawer. If there is no spring, search the back of the drawer aperture for a small protruding piece of tape; if you are lucky enough to find this, pull at it, and the drawer will come out. There might alternatively be a small unobtrusive flat piece of leather unnoticeable unless you look for it to use as a pull. Another favourite spot is inside the well at *the front* (a place in which no one thinks of looking). A whole row of unsuspected small drawers may be hidden here, but they are usually provided with small knobs.

Because secret drawers often lie snugly hidden for years, they are stiff and reluctant to move. Never force them, in doing so you may break a hidden spring. Work on them as gently as possible; when the drawer has been removed, the sides may be rubbed with dry soap or a candle, to ensure easier running in future.

I was once puzzled because the top drawer of the bureau

appeared to me to be considerably smaller from side to side than it should have been. It was an early piece, made before 'cock-beading' was attached to the drawers, pieces of narrow rounded moulding being applied *to the carcase* instead. A wider moulding also ran down the sides, and the whole front was very pretty, yet the outer sides of the bureau where the lopers were seemed to me to be wider than usual. Suspecting a secret drawer I pulled the drawer out, but all seemed normal inside—no sign of springs or pieces of tape. Then it suddenly struck me that usually the spaces where the lopers run are quite open on the inside, but these were tightly closed in by long pieces of wood, which of course terminated on the outside in pieces of rounded moulding to frame the drawer. I pulled gently on one of these, slowly the whole panel slid out, revealing an aperture where all kinds of things could be hidden away without interfering in any way with the running of the loper. It was the same on the other side. Here were my secret drawers! The lady who sold us the bureau had no idea that it contained these interesting features, and I think was very disappointed that there had been nothing hidden away in them.

There are many methods devised by wily craftsmen of concealing drawers in a bureau, I have revealed the secret of some of them, but to go on doing so would be a pity. It will be so much more interesting for the reader to find them for himself. Do not expect to find anything in the drawer when it has been discovered, I have rarely found anything of interest or value in a secret drawer. A dealer friend of mine, however, having spent much time and patience in discovering the whereabouts of one in an ancient bureau he had just purchased, was at last rewarded. On the pressure of a spring, the drawer shot out—at the bottom was a folded piece of paper. With fingers that must have been shaking with excitement he unfolded it, to read two words, 'Sorry Chum!'

CHAPTER EIGHT

Cupboards

CLOTHES CUPBOARDS

Wardrobes

These are the largest type of cupboards, and perhaps one of the earliest. The word comes from the old French, meaning simply 'guard-robe' a place to keep clothes of consequence, away from the ill-effects of dust, moth, damp, etc.

In the days when everything had to be done by hand, from the shearing of sheep, the washing, dyeing, spinning and weaving of the wool, to the cutting and tailoring, clothes were valuable possessions. They had to be carefully preserved, for they had to last a very long time, and in many cases passed on to a succeeding generation. Some clothes, as we have learnt, were folded neatly and kept in chests, but bulky and costly robes trimmed with fur and jewels must be hung up to avoid creasing. This was especially so with regard to the royal robes. These were too numerous even for hanging cupboards, and it is an historic fact that Edward III took over an old mansion in Carter Lane near St Pauls, and had it converted to hold his robes of state. The place it was in was then called 'Wardrobe Court', and the church of St Andrew, which backed on to it, was called 'St Andrew-by-the-Wardrobe', a name it has been known by ever since, although the wardrobe went long ago, and the church itself was burnt down during the Great Fire, and rebuilt in 1692.

But for the ordinary people large oak wardrobes had to suffice. And by some freak of circumstance several, even those of the Gothic period, survive to this day. They were well and beautifully made, but when more up-to-date receptacles for clothes were introduced, they were consigned to the kitchen quarters, or even the stables, and disguised under many coats of paint, go unnoticed until an expert happens to spot them. One such early cupboard was found not long ago in, of all places, Winchester Cathedral. For years it had stood in the middle of a row of painted Victorian cupboards, in a side chapel used as a choir vestry, in which was housed the choir's cassocks and surplices. This attracted the notice of a craftsman employed by the cathedral as a keeper of the wood-work. He noticed that this particular cupboard did not match its neighbours in anything but colour. On closer examination he recognised it for what it was, and with some excitement set to work to have it stripped. Ultimately it was discovered to be a carved oak cupboard of the medieval period. The hinges were intact, and some of the original green paint on the inside. The carving on the outside had been filled in with putty to make the surface smooth and easier to paint, and many successive coats of paint had completely disguised it. Fortunately the paint had marvellously preserved it, and it is now back in the chapel for everyone to admire.

We once bought a fine Gothic cupboard which had come straight out of the kitchen quarters of an old castle in Cornwall. This had always been kept scrubbed, and was a lovely oatmeal colour. Strangely enough it had escaped the notice of both the auctioneers and the experts who attended the sale for the fine oak in the rest of the castle. Perhaps they had never thought of penetrating into the kitchens!

But if one is not lucky enough to find a Gothic wardrobe, there are certainly those of the seventeenth century still on the market. Usually they are of dark oak, with butterfly shaped hinges of iron. The largest have a door at each end with a plain panel in the middle. The cupboard goes all the way through without a division, and there should be two rows of pegs at different heights: the top one for adults, and the lower one for children. Sometimes, unfortunately, these pegs have been removed and a more up-to-date clothes rod inserted. Or the cupboard may have had shelves fitted so that it could be used for storage of items other than clothes. These wardrobes are usually fine, beautifully panelled pieces, made by the joiner, perhaps with a little carving in the top of the doors. But as they are made all in one piece, are cumbersome and difficult to move, and suitable only for fairly large halls, they can often be bought at comparatively low prices.

The smaller wardrobe of this period had no middle panel —just the two doors with maybe underneath a couple of deep drawers to take the tall-crowned hats of the period. This type is the forerunner of the clothes-press mentioned next in this chapter, and is quite rare.

The most fascinating wardrobe I have heard of is one mentioned by Vivien Green in her book *English Dolls' Houses*. It was made specially for a little boy, and was in the form of a large dolls' house of the early eighteenth century in painted oak. It had a gabled roof, and was 4ft 8in wide, 5ft 4in high, and 2ft 2in deep. At either end were projecting wings 8in deep, which were really cupboards provided with locks. The left-hand wing contained four drawers, while the right-hand one had four shelves. Running the whole width of the house at the back was a space for hanging clothes, in which pegs were fixed. On it was painted a signature 14in long, with

3in high letters: 'Edmund Joy 1709'. Who would leave his clothes lying about when he had such an enticing cupboard to put them away in?

The Clothes-press

The natural sequel to the seventeenth-century wardrobe was the early eighteenth-century clothes-press. This was made in two parts, the lower being drawers, and the upper a cupboard. The base was slightly broader than the top, and usually terminated in bracket feet. The upper part was filled with a series of shelves on which the clothes were laid. The doors enclosing the shelves often had fielded panels. These clothes-presses were very well made and attractive pieces of furniture, not often met with today. This is unfortunate because they are an ornament to any room, as well as being extremely useful. A very beautiful example is shown in Plate 25.

The Gentleman's Wardrobe

In the late eighteenth century a version of this called a gentleman's wardrobe was very much in fashion. The shape was similar to the early form, except that the two pieces were the same width, and the shelves were movable and had 'tray' sides. They were made mostly in mahogany. Oak ones are rare and, in my view, rather unattractive, because the oak used at that time by cabinet-makers dealing mainly with mahogany was needed chiefly for the interior of drawers, and was of an uninteresting colour with no life in it. Good examples of such pieces should have a brass edge to the right-hand door of the cupboard to avoid warping.

Like the two previous types of clothes cupboards, the shelves have often been removed, and a brass rod fixed at the top to convert it into a hanging wardrobe. They are extremely useful pieces of furniture and, in oak, are quite reasonable in price.

FOOD CUPBOARDS

Livery Cupboards

So much for the keeping of clothes. Cupboards were also used for the keeping of food, when they receive the puzzling name of livery cupboards. (The meaning of this word as applied to a cupboard is still being debated in learned circles.) These livery cupboards—or a great many of them—come from Wales, and her near neighbours. They are not big pieces, but well made of panelled oak. The format is a cupboard in the lower part, then a drawer, then another cupboard, each cupboard having shelves. About half way up the top cupboard is a grill in the door or doors, about eight inches high and composed of turned wood spindles. This was to let air into the cupboard to keep the food fresh. These are useful and interesting pieces, made all through the eighteenth and beginning of the nineteenth century, of a good-coloured oak. Occasionally livery cupboards may be found with drawers in the bottom half—probably a later edition of the original form.

Hutches

The livery cupboard was obviously the outcome of the much more primitive bread hutch, popular in the sixteenth and seventeenth centuries. These hutches were narrow cupboards about two foot high and wider in proportion, containing a shelf, and made in oak and walnut. The whole of the door was barred with wooden spindles or laths, and they were for keeping bread in. They are still to be found in use in some church porches. Gloucester Cathedral has one, and there are three—two Jacobean and one Elizabethan—in St Albans Abbey, which are used every week. In the latter case the loaves are placed in them on Fridays, and collected on Saturdays by the old almswomen of the city. The general idea is that the rich should put in, and the poor should take out.

European versions of these hutches are bigger and more
elaborate, with short legs and a pediment, shaped and carved,
surmounting the actual cupboard.

COURT CUPBOARDS

These, rightly belong to the seventeenth century, and much
has been written about them and their history in books dealing with early oak furniture. The name 'court' is another
puzzle, which it is not necessary to go into here. Our interest
really lies in the eighteenth-century Welsh version called a
deuddarn meaning 'two parts'. I have always thought these
to be extremely useful pieces of furniture, giving a maximum
amount of cupboard room, and having an interesting exterior.
The larger portion is at the bottom and consists of one large
cupboard containing a shelf, enclosed by two doors. The top
part is narrower from back to front allowing of a sensibly
sized shelf outside the doors, usually two, with a panel between
them. A canopy projects over this shelf, ending at either end
with a round or pear-shaped finial. This canopy usually conceals a very handy recess, never guessed at by those unfamiliar
with this particular piece. A small uncarved panelled edition
made of a good-coloured oak can be an attractive and useful
piece of furniture, but for some inscrutable reason English
buyers fight shy of them.

There is a further piece made in three parts called a
tridarn, but this, unless it is exceptionally small, is rather
overpowering in a small house. The price of a good court
cupboard varies enormously, but I would say that an eighteenth-century uncarved one would be equal in value to any
good dresser of the same period.

CORNER CUPBOARDS

These were a very popular eighteenth-century conception,

and as popular now as ever they were, for the demand greatly
exceeds the supply. At first these cupboards were part of the
pine or oak panelling of the room. If made of pine, they were
painted the same colour as the rest of the paintwork, and were
double corner cupboards as a rule, ie two cupboards one on
top of the other, both with double doors in the same style as
the panelling which were left open for display purposes. The
top cupboard was the taller of the two, and the interior was
painted a soft duck-egg blue. The back was rounded, and
the shelves, about six inches wide, ran all round them. The
middle of each shelf was bowed out sufficiently to take a large
piece of porcelain. The top of the interior was domed, and
often carved to resemble a shell. The doors have often been
removed and the hinge marks filled in, to make the cupboard more of a decorative feature.

A waist-high panelled room of the Queen Anne period, in
addition to the corner cupboard, often contained two other
cupboards of the same shape built into the thickness of the
wall on either side of the fireplace, and starting from the top
of the panelling. Sometimes, when an old house has been
demolished, these cupboards come on to the market. They are
not in themselves complete as they have no proper base, but
a simple corner stand of the same kind of wood can be made
for them to fit into, and they will then be very attractive
pieces of furniture.

Later on in the eighteenth century free-standing double
corner cupboards were made of oak. These are usually rather
large, and not suitable for small rooms, but occasionally a
small one turns up, often made all in one piece, and this is a
treasure to be prized.

Hanging Corner Cupboards
Single corner cupboards were made to hang on the wall.
Do not be surprised if round holes are found in the sides of

these cupboards: when they were made such things as 'mirror-plates' were unknown, and so the cupboard itself was screwed to the wall. The interiors are rarely of oak, which would make the cupboard too heavy for hanging, but of pine, painted originally in a darkish blue. If the cupboard has come from Wales, then it may be papered, because the Welsh liked to paper their cupboards with the same wall-paper as the room. I have removed as many as five layers of wall-paper from a cupboard.

The shelves in a single corner cupboard are usually the same dimensions as the bottom, though they may have prettily carved-out fronts. They were primarily not made for display, but to store the best tea-service in, this being much too valuable to keep in the kitchen. Occasionally one comes across a corner cupboard with one or more drawers at the base, either inside or outside the door.

Country-made hanging corner cupboards were mainly of oak, with one or two doors, depending on their breadth. The doors had fielded panels, sometimes inlaid with a walnut or mahogany banding. Brass 'H' hinges were used on the earlier ones, the later kind having internal hinges. When, very rarely, a bow-fronted pine corner cupboard is found, it is more than probable that originally it was a fine lacquered piece from which the lacquering has peeled away through damp and neglect. But by now the pine has darkened with age and waxing, and is really a lovely pale walnut colour. The cupboard may even be of the rare early type that had scalloped sides at the very top of the structure, containing two tiny shelves. If the original hinges are still in place, they will be of the brass 'butterfly' type.

Bow-fronted cupboards were also made in oak, but not often, for oak does not 'bow' easily, and may even crack if pushed too far. Sometimes, instead of a single piece of wood, narrow wooden strips glued together are used to make the

Plate 21 (*above*) Late seventeenth-century knee-hole desk, with unusual elongated ball feet

Plate 22 (*right*) Writing-desk with folding top (a country edition of the bachelor-chest). Over it is a walnut cushion mirror

Plate 23 (*above*) Very
small early eighteenth-
century oak bureau
with original brasses;
above it an unusual
type of Welsh
spoon rack

Plate 24 (*right*) Early
eighteenth-century
child's oak bureau,
with well-constructed
interior, having two
secret drawers

door, the strips being fastened at the top and bottom to curved pieces of wood. Original glass doors are rarely found on country-made corner cupboards, but belong to the more sophisticated mahogany cabinet-makers' pieces.

SPICE CUPBOARDS OR CABINETS

These charming little cupboards are rare, because they were only in use for a short time—from about the end of the seventeenth century to about 1720. Prior to this period spices were stored in wooden receptacles—beautifully shaped and polished containers, which frequently are impregnated with the scent of the spices they once contained. Spices were brought back from the Dutch East Indies—the 'Spice Islands' so called. This in early days was a very costly procedure, so they had to be kept under lock and key in the living room, and doled out to the cook as they were needed, not so much to flavour the meat, but to disguise its taste, for it was often far from fresh.

The earliest spice cupboards were made of oak, perhaps inlaid with holly or yew. Then came those with 'oyster' walnut decoration on the doors. Oystering was done by cross-cutting thin pieces, for use as veneers, from the root or bough of a tree. These had the appearance of oysters, hence the name. These were quite small cupboards, easily carried about. The doors were provided with locks and keys, and when opened, disclosed rows of little drawers to hold cinnamon, mace, nutmeg, ginger, pepper and cloves.

As the eighteenth century progressed, the cabinets became larger, one or more alcoves being provided to hold a delft jar or lignum vitae receptacle. The workmanship now seems to have been concentrated on the inside of the cabinet—secret drawers were even fitted in some of them—the door as a rule being plain, so that nowadays one finds that it has often been

G

removed altogether, as the piece is more attractive without it.

At this time important country houses were being provided with ice houses—semi-underground chambers in the grounds, where ice was put in during the winter months to remain frozen through the summer, keeping meat and game fresh until it was needed. But bigger quantities of fresh meat were now available in the towns, spices were becoming cheaper to import, and therefore not so valuable, and they could be kept in kitchen cupboards. The spice cupboard became a thing of the past, and those that were left were put to other uses. The Dutch, for instance, were said to keep valuable bulbs in them, and indeed this would seem to be true, for we once bought one which had a label stuck on each drawer, bearing in faded handwriting the names of the bulbs it had obviously once contained.

CARVING ON FURNITURE

As so many of the cupboards, etc, I have mentioned in this chapter are embellished with carving, this seems to me to be as good a place as any, to say something on the subject. Much Welsh furniture of the eighteenth century was still being carved when carving had gone out of date in England. (The items mentioned in this book, though made in the late seventeenth and eighteenth centuries, could really have belonged to an earlier period altogether.)

Carving on any piece, whatever its origin, should always be examined carefully; it is not always what it seems. In the mid nineteenth century many ladies of leisure took it into their heads to learn wood-carving—with disastrous results. Finding oak pieces pushed away in attics and schoolrooms, with lovely plain surfaces fairly asking to be carved, they set to work to embellish them. The lids of bureaux, fronts of chests and coffers, dresser drawer-fronts, edges of tables, all suffered from their efforts, and many a fine piece of furniture has been completely ruined by their ministrations. An expert can tell at a glance, but a novice is 'put out' and puzzled by something he feels is 'not quite right' about the carving.

There are several kinds of early carving, and one should try to familiarise oneself with them; but in many cases these have been copied, so what is to be done? First of all *feel* the carving. Early original carving, from long years of wear and polish, is quite smooth to the touch. Victorian carving is sharp and harsh.

Having carved up plain mid-eighteenth-century pieces made of brown oak, the ladies then had them stained black and French polished—no wonder the learner gets worried! Luckily, instinct will often come to the rescue. The pieces will look wrong anyhow so, if still in doubt and no expert is on hand to advise, avoid them. French polish is something to be avoided. Oak, fruitwood or walnut antique furniture should *never* be French-polished. A wax, either bees-wax or vegetable, should always be used, even if it takes longer to achieve a polish.

Another thing to be avoided with any antique furniture is silicon polish. This is perfectly proper for modern finishes, but certainly not for anything made prior to 1830.

CHAPTER NINE

Small Standing Articles

REVOLVING TABLES

Dumb Waiters

These pieces of furniture are as useful now as when they were first made in the early eighteenth century. They were of English origin, but later were adopted by French and Germans. Made mainly in mahogany and Virginian walnut, there were also a few made in oak. They consisted of three graduated circular trays which revolved round a central pillar mounted on a tripod base. Sometimes a very small fixed tray was placed on the top. The object of the table was that one could turn any tray round until the desired object came within reach. They carried additional plates, glasses, silver, etc, as well as dessert and cheese, and were usually placed near the hostess at the end of the table.

Table Stands

Smaller types of such tables working on a low circular base, and having only one tray, were made to go on tables. Small ones with fitments for cut-glass bottles with an elegant brass, silver, or Sheffield-plate handle on the top were used as CRUET-STANDS. Another type with one, or even two tiers, was fitted with wooden egg-cups and the holes for spoons. These were known as EGG-STANDS.

A third and larger type had only one tray. This held not only the cruets, but butter, jam and marmalade at breakfast, and various sauces and condiments at dinner. It stood in the middle of the table, and ideally the tray was large enough for anyone seated at table to reach it, give it a turn, and take anything that was needed from it, instead of having to ask for it to be passed to him. This piece, made in different kinds of woods, is called a LAZY SUSAN.

Book-tables

Another form of these round revolving tables, was used in libraries as a BOOK-TABLE. The shape was exactly the same as a dumb-waiter, but each shelf was divided by four partitions, which held the books securely in place. This table was most handy for placing by the side of a library chair, when books were needed for reference. The reader could get what he wanted without having to leave his seat. The earliest I have come across was a very elegant one made in oak, with the flattened tripod legs of the William and Mary period.

SPINNING WHEELS

These, too, have their place in a book on country furniture. One very rarely sees them offered for sale now, but there were three main kinds:

1 An early form, still used in Wales for spinning thread for hand-woven tweed, though probably out of doors, as it would be too large for the small-roomed cottages. This type had a long body on four stump legs, easily renewable, like those on the early stools and tables, with a very

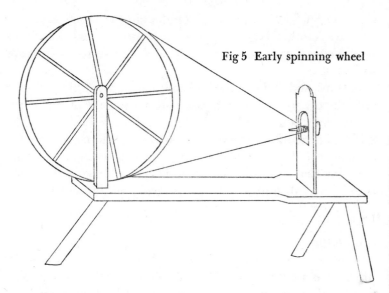

Fig 5 Early spinning wheel

large wheel at one end (Fig 5). The spinner stood to spin, and manipulated the large wheel by hand.

2 A later form worked by a treadle, so that both hands were free to manipulate the thread (Fig 6). This is the kind usually pictured in the story of *The Sleeping Beauty* who pricked her finger on the spindle and slept for a hundred years. The spindle, in any spinning wheel, was the stick on to which the wool was wound. It was made of a hard wood like ash and it's hard to understand how the princess managed to prick her finger on it. It would have been more understandable had she done it on the distaff, which was the long stick that held the wool or flax that had to be spun. It could be any kind of a stick, from one picked out of a hedge, probably forked at the end, to a finely carved boxwood specimen.

3 A third, smaller, and more elaborate kind of spinning wheel, used by the ladies of the eighteenth century for

spinning their sewing cotton or embroidery silk on. As these were used in the beautifully furnished drawing rooms of the period, they were very fine cabinet-makers' pieces, fashioned in beech, yew, satinwood or box, with ivory finials. Pictures of these are sometimes seen in 'Conversation Pieces'. They were small enough to stand on tables, or they had stands specially made for them. Very pretty to look at but irritating things to dust! If something like this is being sought as an 'eye-catcher', I would recommend a wool-winder (Plate 26) which is much less complicated and quite as attractive.

Fig 6 Later spinning wheel

SPINNING CHAIRS

One sees these very rarely, and I think they are interlopers from abroad. The average spinner in this country would have used a stool, or a low chair, I feel sure. The spinning-chair is an attractive shape, with a low seat into which four legs were thrust and kept in position with wedges. The back consisted of a board about eight inches wide and two feet long. This narrowed towards the bottom, where there was a projection of some four inches wide with two holes through it, which fitted into a corresponding slit in the seat. In the thickness of the back of the seat were two more holes. Through these four holes two stout pegs were thrust, thus keeping the back in position.

The back-board had a hand-hold cut in it at the top, and was removable for two reasons. Firstly, it could easily be dismantled for easy transport when there was a spinning-session in the neighbourhood. Secondly, when needed it could be used as a 'washing-bat' for beating the water out of clothes before mangles were invented. This shaped washing-bat is usually Dutch or Scandinavian.

A small, dainty type of this chair stained an 'old oak' colour, and with a highly-carved back-board, found its way into many an Edwardian drawing-room. Beware of these—they are *not* genuine spinning-chairs.

WINDERS

Wool Winders

The most popular—and picturesque—are like the one pictured in Plate 26. This was a large wheel minus its rim, with horizontal spindles attached to each spoke. The wheel was mounted on a pillar, ending in a lidless box on stump feet which held the wool. The wheel was turned by means of a little turned-wood handle fixed to one of the spokes. It is ornamental, and easy to dust, and makes a good decorative piece for a corner. It is useful for winding skeins of wool into balls, although its original use was to wind the spun wool into skeins. Coloured balls of wool can be heaped in the box part, or a liner can be inserted, and flowers put there instead.

Another form, and still decorative, if brightly coloured wool is wound round the reels, is the standing one consisting of a pole, mounted in a weighted wooden base, to which two large wooden reels are attached horizontally by means of metal collars, which slip over the pole and are secured by screws—a similar fitment to that used on pole-screens to hold the fire-screen. The width of the skein can then be wound to any size.

Lace-bobbin Winders

In lace-making districts in England, another kind of thread-winder is found, called a lace-bobbin winder. This stands on a table, and consists of a flattish wooden box with a drawer. At the right-hand end of this is attached a grooved fly-wheel fitted with a belt and knob for turning. This belt works the bobbin-winder on the left-hand side of the box. The thread is drawn from a cross bar in which are holes at intervals for the pegs round which the thread is wound on to the lace-bobbins. The bobbin-holder is made large enough to take a paper or rag packing, to preserve the 'spangled' (ie those with bead rings) lace-bobbins from damage. The cross-bar thread-holder is removable, to make it easy to dismantle the bobbin-winder to carry it about. Unfortunately many winders have got lost for this reason, and the piece is not perfect (and certainly of no use) without one. The drawer in the main part was used to contain the lace-bobbins.

STANDING RUSH-LIGHT HOLDERS

These consisted of narrow turned poles, mounted on varying kinds of heavy bases and were of lamp-table height. On the top of the pole was a steel attachment—rather like a blunt pair of scissors, between the blades of which a rush-light could be fitted horizontally. By its side was usually a saucer to hold a candle. Some rush-light holders had broad wooden rachets instead of a pole, so that the height of the light could be adjusted at will.

Rush-lights were used in kitchen quarters, or in cottages. They were easier to make than tallow dips and most cottagers could not afford to buy wax candles. The method of making was simple. The rushes were peeled almost down to the pith, and then put into iron troughs in which mutton fat had been melted, until they were thoroughly covered with this substance. They were then taken out and dried. When ready for use they were placed in the holder so that an equal amount projected on either side. If not very much light was needed, one side only was lit. If more light was required, both sides were lit, which meant of course that the light lasted only half as long, hence the meaning of the warning in the proverb 'You can't burn the candle at both ends!'

Glove-maker's Donkey

Another standing implement, not unlike a rush-light holder but shorter, was of seventeenth-century origin and was usually found in the glove-making part of the country round Yeovil in Somerset. This was called a glove-maker's donkey (Fig 7). It consisted of a sturdy, turned, upright pillar of oak not unlike the leg of a joint stool, which was supported by a heavy cross-stretcher at the base. At the top was a steel vice, made of two plates of bowed metal with tiny teeth which fitted into each other when closed. The vice could be opened or closed at will by means of an iron rod joined to one of the plates and operated by a treadle, thus leaving the glove-maker's hands free.

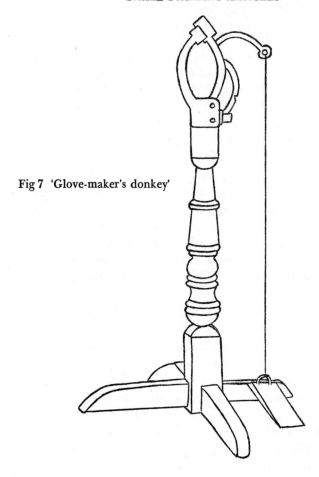

Fig 7 'Glove-maker's donkey'

The glove fingers were in four parts which had to be joined together. Two sides at a time were put in the vice and stitched by hand, the needle going between the teeth that held them, thus ensuring the regularity of the stitches. The thumb was joined in the same way, but afterwards had to be stitched separately on to the glove.

BASIN STANDS

The triangular corner stands, now so popular for holding flower bowls, were cabinet-maker's work, and of mahogany. But there was another variety which was a small square stand, and these are found in oak as well as in mahogany. Four narrow square legs supported the top, which had a basin hole and two holes for soap dishes. (Quite frequently a piece of plain oak has been fitted over the original top, in order to make a bed-side table of the piece.) Halfway down there was a useful drawer, made to hold the towel, and sometimes at the bottom was a cross-stretcher, which had a circle in the middle to hold the jug when the basin was in use—or possibly a small chamber pot. These wash-stands were originally known as 'wash-hand-stands', and that is exactly what they were. They were for use in downstairs cloak rooms for the convenience of visitors.

Another type of basin stand, but for the same purpose, was made in walnut in the early eighteenth century. *Very rarely* one finds them in oak. The design was very simple: three slim turned legs supporting a round frame, big enough to take a bowl about nine inches in diameter, at the top. Halfway down came one or two drawers joining the legs. Near the bottom was a triangular base on tripod legs, ending in pad feet. This platform had a circular place to hold a receptacle— almost certainly a chamber pot—very often a necessity for a visitor in the days before cloak rooms had modern sanitation. The round lidded box that in many cases is found attached to the top of the drawer below the bowl, was made to hold the soap-ball.

Sometimes one hears these pieces called 'wig-powdering stands'. This surely must be a misnomer, because they were only made in the early eighteenth century when powdering had not yet come into fashion. Wigs at that time were composed of long ringlets of natural coloured hair. Later, when powdering was introduced, large 'walk-in' cupboards were provided for those who preferred to wear *their own* hair powdered. I am sure that any wig that needed re-powdering would also be done in such a closet, and not in a bedroom on a beautifully fashioned basin stand much too small for the purpose.

CHAPTER TEN

Clocks and Various Wall-hanging Items

CLOCKS

Let me make it quite clear that I am writing here about CLOCK CASES and DIALS, and not about the works, of which I know very little. But to write a book about country furniture without including such important items as long-case clocks (or 'grandfathers', as they are often called), would be a mistake. Such a clock, whether it goes or not, is always a good addition to any room and seems to give a real welcome in the hall.

The long-case clock in Plate 11 is our own. It was made by Richard Lee of Great Marlow about 1688, and therefore has the right to be considered a piece of country furniture. The top and front are of walnut, the sides of oak. The works are original, and it is in going order. Clocks of this period are rare; but there are, at the time of writing, plenty of oak-cased clocks, and though many have painted faces, there are equally as many with beautiful brass dials. One clock we had, had a most interesting brass dial, without the usual decorative

122

corners. Instead, in these corners, a different view of Plymouth was etched. On the centre of the dial was a ship in full sail, and as well as giving the time, date, and phases of the moon, it also gave the times of high tide in Plymouth Harbour. Old clock cases are often quite beautifully inlaid, and the 'bonnets' on the clocks, with their brass finials, are important-looking.

Brass faced clocks are considered to be more valuable than those with painted faces, but for a country cottage I think the latter are delightful. Pine-cased clocks often have brass faces which look too good for the case. They were probably originally lacquered and the lacquer, degenerating through time and neglect, has ultimately disintegrated, and the case has therefore been stripped down to the pine.

It is no uncommon thing to find that a clock has not always belonged to the case it is now in. One reason for this is that about twenty years ago, in certain districts, country clocks were bad sellers. The works were therefore removed, and the clock case made into two separate pieces of furniture: the glass-fronted top was given a shelf, and the name of 'china cabinet'; the lower half received two shelves, and was dignified with the name 'antique drinks-cabinet'. I have seen many beautiful long-case clocks ruined by this senseless vandalism. The clock works were thrown out on the scrap-heap, unless a nearby clock-maker was interested, and then the cases were mutilated. Now, of course, there is a demand for long-case clocks, and a great shortage of good antique clock-cases; consequently it is possible that a fine case which contained an inferior clock is used for housing a fine clock that has lost its original case.

The 'wag-on-the-wall' type of clock, which had a painted dial without a hood and the pendulum and weight uncovered was, I believe, of Dutch origin and now seems to have disappeared entirely. This is a pity, because it was a cheerful and bright addition to a room. But there is another kind of

clock, to hang on the wall, that can still be found. It was made
with a hood, but the weight and pendulum were exposed.
In the hood there was an alarm. It was described in country
circles as a POST-BOY'S CLOCK, and was made in the latter
part of the eighteenth century. When we acquired one not
long ago, we were warned by the owners that, although the
alarm was in full working order, they never used it because
it alarmed not only the whole household but half the neighbourhood as well! So we handed it on without making the
experiment.

American Clocks

These were actually imported to this country in the middle
of the nineteenth century, but not for long, because their
cheapness was a threat to British clock-makers. They were
very popular for country cottages, and were made in hanging
cases about 18in high, with glass fronts. The top half was
occupied with the clock face, while a coloured print filled in
the bottom half. Some were made as mantelpiece clocks, but
by now, I imagine, have all been exported back to their
country of origin.

'Act of Parliament' Clocks

Another form of clock with which we are all familiar is the
one often seen in old coaching inns. This is usually referred
to as an 'Act of Parliament' clock. It is the popular opinion
that large clocks with easy-to-read faces had been made com-
pulsory for coaching inns, by an Act of Parliament, for the
convenience of passengers changing coaches, and had to be
hung on the wall in conspicuous places. But popular opinion
is not always right. The truth of the matter is that in 1797 a
tax was levied on 'every clock placed in or upon any dwelling
house . . . office, or building whatever, which shall be kept by
any Person or Persons in Great Britain'. This was bad enough,

Plate 25 (*right*) Early
eighteenth-century
small oak wardrobe
or clothes-press

Plate 26 (*below*)
Standing wool-winder
and eighteenth-century
yew-tree Windsor
armchair

Plate 27 (*above*) Watch-case of inlaid mahogany in the form of a long-case clock. Other treen articles are (left to right) snuff-box, Scottish quaich (drinking cup), coffee-grinder and, *in front*, carved snuff-rasp in the shape of a fish, and coquilla nutmeg-grater. Plate 28 (*below*) Watch-case in finely carved mahogany, believed to have belonged to William IV when Duke of Clarence. The crest on the left is thought to be that of Admiral S. H. Bickerton, and on the right that of Rear Admiral Bradley.

and hit those too poor to own a watch, and who had to rely
on other people's clocks, very hard. But watches were also
taxed—gold watches at 10s (50p), and silver or other metal at
2s 6d (12½p), and those who made or sold clocks and watches
were taxed as well.

Two and sixpence in those days was a lot of money, and
ten shillings tax on a gold watch must have seemed outrageous. Consequently people, other than the wealthy, stopped
buying and wearing them. Landlords of coaching inns therefore, at their own expense, had a large clock installed so that
everyone would know the time, and no coaches would be
missed. This was not altogether altruistic; it acted as a good
advertisement, for the clocks became so popular that, when
the tax was rescinded a year later, the inns went on supplying them. In many cases they have continued to keep them
in working order to this day. The last time I visited Helston
in Cornwall, I noticed a fine example of this sort of clock in
the Angel Hotel.

These clocks were about two feet in diameter, with very
big black dials with gilt figures and hands. The frames round
the dial were not very wide, and usually octagonal in shape.
Underneath the dial was a short narrow case to hold the
weights and pendulum.

A smaller type of this clock with a white face, and black
hands and figures, was made in large quantities for the kitchens of large private houses, to ensure the punctuality of
the servants. And a smaller size still was made with well
decorated frames. Sometimes the frames were of mahogany or
rosewood inlaid with brass, sometimes even, of papier-maché
inlaid with mother-of-pearl. These are handsome enough to
hang up in a country-house living room, but for some inscrutable reason, although the cases are of fine workmanship the
faces are uncompromisingly plain.

None of these clocks are what one might term mantelpiece

H

clocks. These *were* made of course, but are mostly Victorian and rather ornate, under glass domes—not really suitable for using with country furniture.

Carriage and Travelling Clocks

These are so simple that they would not look out of place anywhere. The brass framed variety, that is so popular, should really be termed a travelling clock for they were made to take about on one's travels, or even to carry about from room to room—hence the handle on the top. Carriage, or sedan-chair clocks, were actually more like very large pocket watches framed in some suitable way, and were suspended by the ring on the top.

Watches and Watch Cases

Antique pocket watches such as hunters and half-hunters, make admirable mantelpiece clocks when hung in decorative cases specially made for the purpose. There were many varying kinds of these popular items made in all kinds of materials and they were introduced in the eighteenth century to stand watches on at night. Put on the night table by the bed, they did duty as clocks, and only went out of fashion when the Victorian beadwork watch-pockets came into vogue.

Watch cases like miniature long-case clocks (Plate 27) are fascinating. They were true models. Sometimes they were made in the solid, with a hole where the clock face would come. Above the hole at the back was a hook to hang the watch on. Often there was a drawer at the back of the middle part of the clock, for the watch-chain to repose in, and one I saw had a secret drawer in the base, worked by a spring, which was a receptacle for rings. If anyone is fortunate enough to possess an antique watch, a watch case like this makes a most attractive addition to the mantelpiece in any room. The one in Plate 28 gives an idea of how handsome they can look.

Though this watch-case can hardly be described as country-made, it might easily have been made by a clever wood-carver working in the Navy. Beautifully made of mahogany it had a drawer in the base for rings, fobs, seals, etc. This watch case is believed to have belonged to Prince William, Duke of Clarence (afterwards William IV), when he was in the Navy as it bears his Arms. As can be seen from the illustration, the aperture for the watch was under the canopy, and surrounded by the Royal Coat of Arms. It must date prior to 1801—before the Union of Ireland with Great Britain—as only the rose and thistle are featured in the carving. The crests on the left-hand side of the drawer are thought to belong to Admiral Sir S. H. Bickerton, and those on the right to Rear Admiral Bradley who both served with the prince.

BAROMETERS

Barometers, like clocks, were specialised objects, and rarely found framed in oak until well into the Victorian period. A barometer case held as a rule three instruments: the weather glass, the thermometer, and the hydrometer. Usually the case was shaped in one of three ways: like a sign-post, like a stick or like a banjo. It was an instrument intended for use in town houses in the hall, solely for the pleasure of the master of the house, who would tap the glass, adjust the indicator, and then be guided by what he had seen as to whether a walking stick or an umbrella would be the most suitable article to take out with him on his way to his club or office.

From the fact that, unlike clocks, country woods were not used to make the cases, one deduces that the country squire or farmer preferred to use his own judgement and that barometers were not needed in his house at all. There was the weather-vane on the barn or the stables as well as all the out-door portents, while for the females of his establishment there was the salt-box in the kitchen, a bit of seaweed on a hook in the back lobby, and the primitive WEATHER HOUSE in the nursery. These amusing devices did not, like the cuckoo clocks, all come from Switzerland. Some crude early nineteenth-century ones were of country make, and the weatherman and his wife were represented by figures very much resembling Noah and his wife. They worked on cat-gut, which is affected by the weather (Plate 29).

MIRRORS

These came to be used for decoration in Jacobean times. They were quite small in size, and were framed in small bits of glass leaded together, or in pine frames covered with needlework, with thin walnut outer frames.

Later, the 'cushion' mirror made its appearance. The frame of this was well rounded and made of walnut or laburnum, and 'oystered' if possible. As lacquer furniture was now in fashion, there were also lacquer-framed mirrors. In the early eighteenth century, walnut frames were inlaid with seaweed marquetry (Plate 22). This delicate interlaced design, though originating in Italy, was brought to perfection by English craftsmen. Most of these mirrors were finished at the top with a 'crest'—a piece of carving similar to those on Carolean chairs—sometimes, though not necessarily, incorporating the crest or initials of the purchaser. Plainer types of this mirror, made either to stand or hang, and without the crest, were called 'BARBER'S' MIRRORS. One supposes they were part of the barber's stock-in-trade, together with the special basins made with a piece cut out of the wide brim to fit round the neck. These basins were made in delft, copper or pewter. At a later period Wedgwood made them in his famous cream ware, with jugs to match.

But none of these mirrors is suitable for use with the later type of eighteenth- or early nineteenth-century country furni-ture. It is a curious thing that very few mirrors seem to have been used in small country houses, apart from dressing-table looking-glasses. The best known types are:

Gilt overmantel mirrors usually with three panels of glass framed in a plainish gilt frame, sometimes rather architectural in character. These were primarily in-tended to reflect the light of the mantelpiece candles, thus doubling their power.

Longish gilt-framed mirrors, often with a picture in the top, also slightly architectural in form. These, like the overmantels, were meant to be fixed to the wall, and not hung. Their proper place was between two windows to act as a pier glass.

Neither of these mirrors is what one needs for a special place in a dark room to reflect light, or give a delightful glimpse of a colourful garden. (Hence, by the way, the name 'mirror', which I think implies that it was not necessarily meant to be used for looking at oneself in). If one is looking for a mirror to go with country furniture, sometimes a plain gilt convex mirror can give a fascinating effect, and does not look amiss. Or antique picture frames made of walnut, or those of carved or moulded pine, are sometimes the answer (Plates 8 and 12), fitted with an old piece of Victorian mirror-glass. Do *not* use modern glass, it looks all wrong. The back is no longer 'silvered' as it used to be, and the 'depth' of old glass is therefore lost. Victorian glass, (taken from old over-mantels or looking-glasses) is not difficult or expensive to obtain, and well worth the effort of searching for. Care must be taken, not to choose too heavy a glass if the frame is fragile.

The papier-maché clock frames, mentioned previously (page 127), also make excellent mirror frames if well decorated and in good condition. The back, which held the works, of course must be removed first.

CUTLERY CONTAINERS

Spoon Racks

While we are on the subject of objects to hang on the wall, it would be as well to give a description of spoon racks. There are two forms of these, each quite different from the other. The first and earliest is the Welsh variety which consists of a rack made like an inbuilt succession of steps—each step having holes in it to take six spoons. As these holes are round, they were obviously intended for wooden spoons. These racks were made to be hung on the wall. The back was shaped upward in a curve, and the front panel cut away in a primitive design to show the handles of the bowls of the spoons, and the handles of those on the bottom shelf are plainly visible. No kitchen in Wales would have been without one of these useful objects (Plates 4 and 23).

The other kind (Plate 11) were made in the north of England in the eighteenth century and were meant more for the dining room than the kitchen. They were specially designed to show off the shape of the entire spoon and the sides of the back and top were usually carved out in a graceful way. I do not think they were intended for pewter spoons, but for silver ones, and when used for this purpose make most attractive wall pieces. At the bottom of the rack was a box, either with or without a lid, intended for the knives or forks. Such racks were invariably made of oak.

Knife Boxes

A companion to the spoon rack was the hanging knife box. This was a long narrow box, much wider at the top than the bottom. It had a shaped back, rising above the box part, and a sloping lid. These boxes were made of oak inlaid with mahogany, or of mahogany or fruitwood. Sometimes the latter had a design of a knife and fork inlaid with boxwood on the front. They were made wider at the top to take the heavy curved silver handles of the knives.

Cutlery Boxes

There is another variety of hanging box, consisting of a long, fairly wide back panel on which two lidless boxes are fixed leaving a plain piece in the middle between the two. I think it may have been a cutlery box, where the spoons were kept in the top and the knives in the bottom. These boxes are very rare.

The other type of cutlery or knife box was not made to hang but this is perhaps the best place to mention it. Made in both oak and mahogany, such boxes date from about 1760, and have most attractively scalloped edges in the Chippendale manner. There is a division down the middle, slightly higher than the sides, in which is a 'handle-hold'. They were meant to hold knives, and were kept on the sideboards and dressers of the less wealthy household. If not used for this purpose now they make unusual receptacles for flowers, using low containers so that the heads of the flowers do not hide the beauty of the cut-out sides and ends.

CANDLE BOXES

These were rather like knife boxes with straight sides. They were used for the conservation of candles, and hung at the side of the fireplace in each living room. The lids were made to slide upwards so that the candles could be taken out *from the bottom*, thus preserving the wicks. Every kind of wood, including padouk, was used for the making of these boxes. For some time in the eighteenth century there was a tax on pure wax candles, which made people treat them with care; they would never be used in the kitchens or domestic quarters for instance. Tallow candles, made of animal fat, would be good enough for these places, and these were kept in long barrel-shaped boxes hung sideways, with a door in the uppermost side. They were made of wood, brass or tin. Strangely enough, this kind of candle box is now much rarer than the more refined type.

SALT BOXES

Some people are inclined to call every wooden box which hangs on the wall a salt box irrespective of what shape it is, or what it is made of.

Actually a salt box was a most uninteresting large utilitarian box made of plain unadorned oak or sycamore, which was hung where it would be most needed—at the side of the kitchen fire-place. They were in constant use, and one can always recognise them by the fact that it is impossible to get a polish on the lower part of the box where the salt actually lay. These boxes are all right when kept in a dry place, but moved from the fire-place a white rim, or even a thin layer of salt, will form on the outside of the box in damp weather, due to the wood having become thoroughly impregnated with the salt.

GLOVE BOXES

A box, rather like a salt box, but with a drawer in the base, was used as a handy receptacle for almost anything and was kept on the hall table. It is usually referred to as a 'glove box', the idea being that it held gloves meant for wear on country walks one supposes. These are still found on hall tables in country houses, often used for keeping odd bits of string in the top and scissors in the drawer underneath, and very useful they are when there are parcels to be done up. They were usually made of oak with a carved piece at the top of the rising lid. The drawer was inlaid round the edge with walnut banding, and furnished with brass knobs.

Another form of glove box, for hanging on the wall, was of a longish narrow shape. The back was extended upwards behind the lid, and had a pierced hole in the centre for hanging purposes. The lid sloped down from back to front.

CHURCH-WARDEN PIPE RACKS

There were two simple hanging varieties of these—one, similar in size, and shaped somewhat like a Yorkshire spoon-rack but with sides that started narrow at the top, and increasing in width as they reached the bottom. In the right-hand side spaces were cut about three inches apart, to take the stem of the pipe nearest to the bowl, the bowl then hung *outside* the rack. In the left-hand side a round hole was cut to take the mouth-piece end of the pipe, which was thrust through it, so that the pipes lay across the box and each was easy to remove without disturbing the other. At the bottom was a lidless box, meant I suppose to hold individual tobacco boxes. These racks were made mostly of mahogany. The second kind was a long narrow-sided rack about fifteen inches high with several divisions going lengthwise. It had a top and bottom, but no back. A wide piece of wood went from side to side across the front of the box to hold the bowls of the pipes, which stood upright between the divisions.

Even empty, these racks make interesting wall pieces, and are eye-catchers with all the pipes in place. They were mid-eighteenth century, usually made of oak.

Perhaps the most obvious things one would expect to find hanging on the walls of country houses are

WARMING-PANS

There were three different types of these: brass-faced pans, copper pans, and a later, nineteenth-century version of the latter.

Brass-faced Pans

These were the earliest kind, and originally had long steel handles, either flat, or rounded like a poker. The ember pan at this time was either of iron or bronze, with a brass covered rim, and the lid was very much bigger, and did not fit the pan, but hung over it.

It was in one of these seventeenth-century warming pans that the baby was supposed to have been smuggled into the queen's bed, when the long-hoped-for heir was being born in James II's reign. That this canard was started by a male courtier attendant at the scene with no more than a cursory knowledge of warming-pans or babies, is quite evident—it would be an impossibility to cram a normal sized infant into such a space. Obviously he imagined the pan to be the same size as the cover. The brass warming pan with a wooden handle continued until well into the eighteenth century.

Copper Pans

These are typical of the eighteenth and early nineteenth century and were made of copper throughout. The pan had a rim into which the lid fitted tightly, and these lids were well decorated, though constant polishing has by now almost obliterated the design. The whole of the pan, not just the face, was kept clean and bright when it was in use, for after it was filled with embers it was rubbed up and down the bed between the sheets, and a dirty pan would have been ruinous to the bed-linen.

Later in the nineteenth century someone hit upon the bright idea of sealing the lid to the bottom of the pan, making a small hole in the middle of it and fitting it with a screw-on stopper; the warming-pan could then be filled with hot water instead of live embers. This must have been done when kitchens were fitted with ranges, and the open fires, from which the embers had hitherto been taken had become things of the past.

A short time elapsed, and then another idea was tried—that of screwing the handle into the pan, so that it could be unscrewed, leaving the pan in the bed to continue the warming process. In this case, the handle also was made of metal, and was fitted at the end with a ring for hanging-up purposes. From this copper pan to stone hot-water bottles was a short step.

When buying a warming-pan, particular attention should be paid to the wooden handle, for this can be quite an important asset. A fine warming-pan had a well turned handle, often made of a lovely coloured fruitwood which looks extremely well when hanging on the wall. Accidents have happened to these original handles from time to time and replacements have been made, with nothing more exciting than a broomstick. This may have acquired a fine patina through the years, but at least half of the artistic interest is lost.

CHAPTER ELEVEN

Beds and Their Furnishings

The bed has been through the ages, an important, if not *the* most important article of furniture in the house. Perhaps the Tudor and Stuart times saw it at its most splendid—but as these splendid beds were made for affluent and important personages, we are not so much concerned with them as with those that came into fashion in the eighteenth century, known familiarly as 'Four-Posters'. These were a simplified form of the early oak ones, which had consisted of four posts, heavily carved. The two at the head held between them a massive carved head board. These posts and the two at the foot of the bed supported a canopy of carved, panelled or painted oak called a 'tester'. There was no foot-board to the bed—indeed very often the two foot posts stood some way away from the bed itself, probably to make room for the highly ornate coverlet. The head board often had a small secret cupboard concealed in the panelling where personal treasures could be safely hidden while the owner slept. The eighteenth-century term 'four-poster' was really a misnomer, because the only posts that showed were those at the foot of the bed, those at the head being hidden by hangings. These beds were made both in oak and mahogany. If of oak the bottom posts were turned in a simple manner, if of mahogany, then they were carved in the prevailing fashion of the period. Hepplewhite period posts for instance were slender and delicately carved, tapering considerably towards the top. The heavy wood tester had now been replaced by a light cornice going round three sides of the top of the bed. On this was nailed a piece of material, matching the hangings.

The four-post bed was intended for the master bedroom of the house. In a smaller and less important room we might have found a simple oak bed, probably one remaining from the seventeenth century, consisting merely of a high panelled head board attached to the top end of the bedstead, with no foot posts or curtains. Towards the end of the eighteenth century another simple bed made its appearance. This had four prettily turned posts, with a short head and foot board—there was no tester or curtains.

For those living in small cottages there were cupboard beds containing hay or straw mattresses used for reasons of warmth or privacy. In the humble two-roomed cottages of Wales a tall dresser was often used to divide one of the rooms into two. The top of it served two purposes; that of plate-rack in the kitchen, and bed-head in the bedroom.

The early eighteenth century terrace houses in towns provided the maidservant with a cupboard on the last landing of the staircase, and this did duty for a bed. It ran the width of the back wall and was deep enough to take a straw mattress which was placed on a built-in chest that served to hold the girl's few possessions. She would have to undress on the landing, bundle her clothes into a corner of the cupboard, then climb in herself, closing the door behind her. Air was provided through the top of the cupboard, which was not closed in.

The mahogany four-post beds of the mid-eighteenth century and onwards were ideal for several reasons. One of these was that, though they looked solid enough, they could be taken apart in a matter of minutes for easy moving, and just as easily put together again. First of all, and most important, came the two foot posts, which were turned, and finely carved according to the taste of the carver. The head posts came next, and were often of stained pine and quite plain. These were never seen, as they were covered by the back curtains. The four posts were joined together by two heavy side pieces and a head and bottom piece, which projected into the posts and were screwed there by long bed-screws, which, in the case of the foot posts, were covered with small panels. On the top of the posts were spikes, which supported the carved or moulded cornice which ran round three sides of the bed. Inside the cornice were long metal rods to hold rings for the curtains. At the head of the bed was a head board to support the pillows. The base of early beds was roped (like the big chairs and settles of the period); the ropes going through holes in the four side pieces. The later beds had bed-laths, about four inches wide, which fitted laterally at intervals across the bed, into spaces provided for them in the sides. Each lath and space was numbered to correspond. The ropes or laths held the straw or hair mattress that was the foundation of the bed.

The hangings which surrounded the bed were most important—made of dimity or chintz for the summer, and brocade or velvet for the winter. In Jacobean times they were hand-embroidered in wool on linen or cotton twill. They consisted of the tester—a canopy that not only covered the space at the top of the bed, but hung down behind it—and four curtains called valances, which hung down to the floor. These acted as curtains to the truckle bed if it were used (page 164).

On the straw or hair mattress, was placed the feather bed. Feather beds, especially if made of goose feathers, were very valuable possessions, handed down in the family, or even left as legacies. There was a great art in making the bed, a large one taking two people to do it. First, opposite corners of the feather bed had to be grasped firmly, and the feathers all shaken into the middle. Then they were plumped out evenly, finally being smoothed with a bed-smoother—an implement which consisted of a stick with a flat round piece at the end of it the size of a tea plate.

Having finished smoothing the bed, the bolster was placed across the top end. The bed linen followed beginning with the bottom sheet, neatly tucked in all round and rolled round the bolster, then the down pillows in the cases followed by the top sheet, the end of which was embroidered or hemstitched. This end was turned down over the woollen blankets which came next. Over this came the quilt.

The quilt was made of old soft blankets covered with white cotton material; on the top cover a design was drawn out. The blankets and covers were then stitched together with neat, even stitches which followed the design—this was called 'quilting' and was a great art. Very often the top layer, instead of being plain white cotton material, consisted of a patchwork of various cotton pieces—the remnants from the summer frocks of the female portion of the house. When this was the case it was called a 'patch-work quilt'. In Victorian days silk and velvet pieces were feather-stitched into place, on an interlining which was lined and *not* quilted, this was called a 'bedspread', 'coverlet', or 'counterpane'. Some bedspreads were made of candle-wick worked in intricate designs, candlewick being the tufted white cotton used for making the wicks of candles. American ladies were highly proficient at quilting and bedspread making, and anyone interested in this fascinating craft can see a wonderful collection at Claverton Manor, near Bath, the American Museum in England.

People often say how stuffy our ancestors must have been to curtain their beds so heavily, but one must remember the two things they had in mind when doing so—warmth and privacy. In the very earliest days, the window apertures, or 'arrow slits' were not even glazed, and cold icy winds, not to mention fog, snow and rain, came through them into the room. There was a great need of bed curtains to keep out these elements. A log fire in the fireplace did not heat anything except what was immediately in front of it and, anyhow, would have died down long before morning. A curtained feather bed may be stuffy, but it must have been remarkably soft and comforting in cold weather. As regards privacy, often there were no doors to the upstairs rooms, one led out of another, and often there were no passages or landings: one simply went from one end of the house to the other through a succession of bed-rooms. A certain amount of privacy was necessary, and curtains which would pull close all round a bed provided this.

Later on, when glass was put in the windows, and doors fitted to the rooms, only the side curtains at the head of the bed were pulled at night, mainly to keep out the draughts.

In mid-Victorian times when houses became less draughty the tester was discarded, and the bottom posts were shortened and held a shaped foot board. A half-tester at the top was substituted, and there were two curtains at the head of the bed only. But the bedrooms in large houses could still be icy cold in winter, as they can be even today where no central heating is supplied. I have stayed in hotels where curtains, feather beds, and even warming-pans, would be welcome.

About 1820 the foot posts were much heavier and the carving on them not nearly so fine. And some ten years later the half-tester became more popular than the four poster, and continued to be so until the end of the century.

Plate 29 (*above*) Child's comb-back chair in ash, small oak table holding a lead pump and a weather house of painted wood; all early nineteenth-century

Plate 30 (*left*) Child's eighteenth-century rocking chair in cherry-wood. (This popular shape was made in all kinds of wood)

Plate 31 *(left)* Child's high-chair in cherry-wood; note the unusual 'pierced' ladders. Beside it is an oak tripod wine-table

Plate 32 *(below)* Early oak cradle with unusually shallow hood, giving an almost Gothic effect

CHAPTER TWELVE

Kitchen, Scullery and Dairy Furniture

Up to about fifty years ago the furnishings of country kitchens remained much the same as they had been for centuries— and indeed there may be remote parts of the country where this is still true—but even country kitchens have undergone a great change in recent years, and nowadays this is the one room in the house that people do not contemplate furnishing with antiques. However, a great number of things that were in daily use in kitchens have now found their way into other parts of the house, and are being used for quite other purposes. It would perhaps be a good idea for us to know the real purpose for which such things were made. The nominal kitchen furniture of course would have included the scrubbed pine refectory and cricket tables, pine settles, bacon cupboards, and stools. These have already been mentioned; so have dressers, but I think we might take note of the outsize dressers usually found in the kitchens of big farmhouses and inns.

145

J

Outsize Dressers

These were provided with enormous drawers to take baking tins, and the large ironing-blanket and sheet, also the
iron-stands, used on ironing days. The working tops of
these dressers were usually quite two inches thick, and of
oak (while the rest of the dresser was painted-pine). This
was because it had to be of some strong durable wood, as a
great many things were done at the dresser when the table
was being used for other purposes. The top was always kept
scrubbed, until the beginning of the present century, when
it was usually covered with oilcloth to save the hard work of
scrubbing. The rack of this dresser was also huge, and the
whole piece of furniture was secured to the wall, for it was
really a fixture, and not meant to be moved. It was strictly
utilitarian, and not remarkable for its beauty. I found a good
use for the rack of one of these pieces. It had well graduated
sides, with shelves at wider spaces towards the top. It had no
back, and luckily there were no hooks on the shelves. I
stripped and polished it, turned it upside down, and now it
does duty on the landing as a bookcase, housing all my favourite, and therefore shabbiest, books. Being eighteenth century,
it has a faintly Hepplewhite look and I don't think anyone
would guess what it had once been.

Grain Chests or Bins

These were normally kept in barns and granaries, but
occasionally one comes across one in the kitchen of a farm.
In this case it will be a real piece of furniture and not just
a rough chest. This kind was usually made of elm with
bracket feet, and stood higher than the normal chest. The
main feature was the division down the middle, which meant
that there were two lids, one for each bin. Sometimes these
were provided with locks, and the keyholes were furnished

with brass escutcheons.

Elm is a wood that can achieve a lovely golden colour, and has a well marked grain, so that a solid piece of furniture like a grain bin can be utilised almost anywhere, being as ornamental as it is useful.

Knife-cleaning Board

This is a piece of scullery furniture from Wales. It was made of scrubbed pine and consisted of a long board about eight inches wide. A box is fixed at the bottom of the board to hold chunks of 'Bath-brick', a preparation of sandstone manufactured (originally at Bridgwater) in the form of bricks. The board was laid flat on the table, and a certain amount of brick scraped off on to it, and damped with water or vinegar, and rubbed on to the steel blades of the knives. When all the stains had been removed, the knives were 'honed' up and down the length of the board, and then finished off with a soft duster. The board was hung up on the wall when not in use. English knife boards were not nearly so ornamental. The boards were much shorter and the working side covered with leather. There was no box for the Bath-brick.

Oatmeal or Riddle Boards

These have found their way down country from Scotland and the north of England, and are a puzzle to most southerners. They were made of wood, and roughly about eighteen to twenty inches square, rounded at the top, through which a hole was pierced for hanging purposes. They had a diagonal lattice of indented lines forming one-inch squares, which makes their appearance quite ornamental when hanging on the wall.

These boards were used in biscuit-making, and oatmeal dough was rolled out on them. They did *not* go in the oven, but were just for rolling-out and marking purposes.

Oatmeal Rollers

In conjunction with these boards, short stout rollers were used. These were not smooth like pastry rolling-pins, but had raised squares all round them, for the purpose of crushing the oatmeal. The plain side of the oatmeal boards may have been used for this purpose. Before the days of cooking stoves, baking had to be done in special baking ovens.

Baking Ovens and Dough Bins

These were built of brick, high up at the side of the chimney, and had thick wooden doors, that were just lodged in front of the aperture—or an iron door on hinges. These ovens were deep cavernous affairs into which a large quantity of kindling wood (or dried gorse) was thrust and set alight When the ovens became hot enough to bake in, the ashes were raked out and the bread put in. Cakes, pies and potatoes were also baked in bread ovens. They were removed from the ovens with a flat, spade-like wooden implement, called an OVEN PEEL, the cottage variety of which had a short handle. The same kind of thing was made in iron or steel but with a long handle, for use by bakers, who needed them for their much larger bread-ovens. The open fireplace in the scullery very often housed the bread oven—(instead of it being in the kitchen) and therefore the baking was done here. The dough was set to rise in a piece of furniture called a DOUGH BIN. This was normally made of elm. It was from three to four feet long, and a couple of feet wide, and high enough to work at comfortably. In shape it was a box with canted sides and ends, in other words the base was much smaller than the top, and about eighteen inches to two feet high. The square legs were fixed to the back and front of the bin about half way up. As the bin sloped, the legs had to be shaped to fit it and were then fastened on with wooden pegs.

The top was removable. When in place it did duty as a

table on which to make the dough into loaves. There was an earlier kind made in the seventeenth century, of oak, with turned legs, similar to those on gate-leg tables. The legs were fixed to the bin in the same way, but were joined together near the base with square rails. These are rare, and very desirable. About twenty years ago it was quite possible to buy the elm dough bins at a very reasonable price, and many people did so, to use them as small sideboards or serving tables. But they did not want to have to keep on raising the lid to get at what was stored inside. So they had the top fastened to the bin, a shelf placed halfway down and a door cut in the front—if the bin did not slope too much. There were many of these 'conversions'. But a door in a dough bin that has a fixed top, means that the piece is not original. This may not matter so much in the case of eighteenth-century elm ones, but it would be a sin to convert a seventeenth-century oak one in this manner. Left as they are they make a very good rug-chest for the hall.

Game-carriers

These are interesting and attractive pieces, usually made of scrubbed pine. They consisted of three shelves pegged firmly with wooden pegs into four legs, which were about five feet high. The legs were about three inches square. The back ones were straight, but the front legs sloped out forwards towards the bottom. The top shelf was about twelve or thirteen inches deep and was rimmed all round to prevent any articles placed on it from falling off. Along the front rim was a row of big hand-forged iron hooks on which the game was hung.

The lower shelf was recessed, and of a narrower depth. This had front and side rims, but a board some ten inches high ran along the back, against which plates were presumably lodged. The bottom shelf was fifteen or sixteen inches deep,

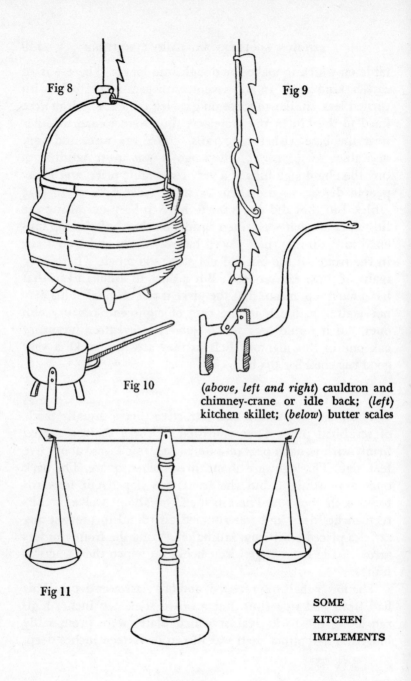

Fig 8

Fig 9

Fig 10

(*above, left and right*) cauldron and chimney-crane or idle back; (*left*) kitchen skillet; (*below*) butter scales

Fig 11

SOME
KITCHEN
IMPLEMENTS

also rimmed. I imagine that these two lower shelves were for the plucked game to rest on.

Bowls

Among the things from the kitchen quarters that are now used in living rooms, are the lovely shallow, wide sycamore bowls, once used for 'setting the cream' in dairies, and the deeper 'mixing-bowl' made of the same wood. Sycamore is a naturally light wood with a fine grain, but years of use have turned it a lovely golden colour, and bowls of this sort are in great demand for flower and fruit holders.

Butter-scales

Originally from the dairy, these are scarce but lovely things for flowers. A wooden pillar, about eighteen inches high, mounted in a heavy block, supports the cross arm from which the scale plates are suspended (Fig 11). These are shaped like deep saucers, and easily contain any ordinary saucer used as a liner. All one has to do is to float a large flower—an open rose, or rhododendron head, with its natural foliage, in each saucer, arranging it so that one scale plate hangs higher than the other. The result is charming.

Coopered Vessels

Coopered vessels of wood were used before galvanised iron had been invented. The work was done by the cooperers, and consisted of wooden staves being driven into holes made in the solid base of the article. These were kept in place by bands of iron, copper, or brass (or in the case of small objects, split willow) placed at regular intervals round the article. The bands were occasionally nailed to the staves to keep them from slipping. These coopered vessels were used for anything liquid; they are still used for beer barrels, water butts or wine casks. But in the eighteenth and early nineteenth centuries they were used for a variety of household utensils such as washing tubs, washing-up bowls, and buckets. And for grander uses such as wine-coolers and 'food-voiders' etc, when they were made of brass-bound mahogany. The idea was that the loose staves would adapt themselves to being alternately wet and dry without warping. Nowadays, when used only for dry purposes, the staves will shrink, and the bands that bind them become loose, and eventually fall out of place, or off the piece altogether.

Washing-up bowls, oval in shape, with extended staves at each end in which handle-holds have been cut, are ideal as plant holders. Washing tubs or pails are useful in the garden for shrubs or bulbs. If used for dry purposes such as log buckets, the bands should be fixed with screws to the wood at intervals, to save them from slipping to the ground. Coopered buckets were used extensively in dairies and stables, but were found too heavy and clumsy to be used as fire buckets. Leather buckets were therefore used for this purpose.

Leather Buckets

These can still be seen hanging in rows in the passages of old country inns. The leather was joined down the side with copper rivets and there was an inner copper ring round the base for additional strength. The handles were made of leather-bound ropes. Leather buckets would also have been found in large mansions, and would have had the owner's crest or coat-of-arms painted on them—just as the name of the inn was painted on those in use there. Before the days of adequate fire services leather buckets were very numerous, but in the twentieth century, having been out-moded by modern fire-fighting appliances, they came on to the market, where they were much in demand for wastepaper baskets or umbrella-stands. In fact so popular did they become that the demand greatly exceeded the supply, and they were then reproduced in large quantities.

Occasionally a genuine one still turns up in a sale, but by now the reproductions have become somewhat battered and knocked about, and are often offered for sale—*and* priced— as being the genuine article, so care should be taken in examining them before paying the large price that the genuine antique ones command.

Pestles and Mortars

Of all antique wooden implements used in a kitchen these are without doubt the most lovely. Although pestles and mortars were made of many materials—iron, bronze, brass, bellmetal, marble, and even glass—wooden ones would seem to have been the most popular. It must be remembered that mincing machines, as we know them, were not invented until well on into the nineteenth century. Therefore up to that date everything that would now be minced, had to be cut up into small pieces with a sharp knife, put into a mortar, and pounded with a pestle. Pestles and mortars have returned to favour lately, Victorian marble ones being very popular for domestic use.

In the old kitchens at least two of these implements would be needed, one kept solely for onions and garlic, for the smell from these pungent plants would impregnate a wooden mortar. The favourite wood for seventeenth-century mortars was lignum vitae. The very large ones were made in this wood, which is so hard that they remain almost as good as new to this day. Another reason for the popularity of lignum vitae was the idea that it had medicinal properties and was therefore a highly suitable wood to use in the preparation of food and drink.

Next in popularity for largish mortars came walnut, and many other woods were also used. This was specially so for the small mortars used in cottage kitchens, which could be made of any wood growing outside the back door. These are so original and charming in shape that it is not surprising they are eagerly sought after by collectors. The large mortars varied very little in shape. They always had to be used on tables and needed large bases to keep them firm and steady when in use, whereas the small kind could be used in the crook of the arm and therefore could be virtually any shape.

Very small mortars of lignum vitae and glass were made for apothecaries for pounding small substances. The lignum vitae ones were cone-shaped, and only three or four inches high. It is rare to find these still containing their pestles. Glass ones usually do, however, because they were put away carefully in medicine cabinets or in the drug-carrying boxes of the doctors.

Pestles especially for the more important mortars were as beautifully shaped as the mortars themselves, and it was said that the sign of a good pestle was that it would balance in an upright position in the mortar. This rarely happens today however as both pieces have become somewhat worn in use.

We cannot leave the kitchen quarters without saying something about one of its most interesting, useful, and often very beautiful adjuncts: coffee mills.

Coffee Mills

When coffee was first introduced into England in the second half of the seventeenth century the beans had to be ground in a mortar. This was a laborious proceeding, which obviously had to be remedied. About 1660 lignum vitae mills for grinding coffee had been invented by a Nicholas Brook of Tooley Street, London—with great advantage to the numerous coffee houses springing up all over the city. By the middle of the eighteenth century they were being made in profusion. The early ones were always made of lignum vitae, but later, other woods were used; and later still, mahogany mills came into fashion. In all cases the mechanism was much the same. The beans were poured into a receiver at the top, and passed from thence into a compartment where the grinder was, and through that into the powder compartment in the bottom of the mill. Each part could be screwed to each other, 'threads' for that purpose being cut in the wood. The handle was hinged, and could be removed from the spindle, folded up and kept, when the mill was not in use, in the bottom compartment.

The shapes of the mills varied. The early ones were vase-shaped, and supplied with screw-on lids to hide the spindle. Then came the more ordinary round shape with a wooden saucer to receive the beans. The latest eighteenth-century type was on a square base which contained a drawer (Plate 27). The folded handle was placed in this drawer when not in use. In the early nineteenth century the receiving bowl was made of brass, and the handle was fixed. The detachable handles must easily have been lost, if not put away immediately after use, for more often than not one finds these mills without handles. Mr Pinto, a connoisseur of the subject, suggested that this was because so many of these eighteenth-century coffee mills had been converted into lamps (the handles being thrown away in the process). But I am convinced that it was the other way about. I have only seen one coffee mill treated in this way over many years, and this was one we converted ourselves because the handle was missing when we bought it, and the mill was useless without it.

CHAPTER THIRTEEN

Children's Furniture

CHAIRS

There were many more chairs made for country children than for those living in towns. The reason is obvious. In the country almost any handyman, given the wood and the tools, could make a chair for a child. In the town it had to be the cabinet-maker who doubtless would make a little masterpiece, but at considerable cost.

One of the easiest, and most useful, country chairs ever made was a Welsh one with a simple heavy chunk of wood for a seat, a rounded narrow back supporting the arms and *no legs!* This chair could be set on the floor for a toddler to sit in, and then transferred to a higher spot, such as another chair, or the table, or even one end of the long stone sink for the baby (not yet old enough to walk) to be wedged in, under the watchful eye of his mother. Father probably made this chair. Although we treasure these old country-made chairs to-day they were not so highly considered when they were made, and when too battered for further use were just thrown out— hence the scarcity of the country child's chair at the present time.

Rocking Chairs

Rocking chairs, often doing double duty as a commode, were the favourites, and these, with one exception, were copies of the chairs adults sat in—ladder-backs, spindle-backs, Windsors, etc. The exception was the wing-armchair illustrated in Plate 30. These are early eighteenth-century shape, as regards the seat, but the 'skirts' of the chair, that are rounded to form rockers, were specially invented for this purpose. Practically all low-chairs are armchairs. Single chairs were made for older children, but are rare.

High-chairs

High-chairs were made, not to sit the baby in just to get rid of him while the mother worked around the house—but for the toddler to sit up to the table in. He was not provided with a tray to this chair, nor yet a stick to keep him in; the heavy oak table at which he sat provided both—a place for his plate and spoon, and an effective means of keeping him in the chair. There was hardly ever a foot-rest. This came at a much later period in the nineteenth century when trays were supplied to hold toys or food, and the baby did not sit to the table any more. One sees many high-chairs where the foot-rest is very obviously of much later date.

High-chairs, like low-chairs, followed prevailing adult designs (Plate 31). A very rare form of high-chair, for use at the table, was one where the legs and back of the chair were the same height as the rest of the set of dining chairs. The part the child sat in was set back on the normal seat of the chair, the protruding edge of which formed a foot-rest. There is a seventeenth-century oak high-chair of this kind, the back inlaid with holly and bog-oak, in the Victoria & Albert Museum.

In the middle of the eighteenth century another form of high-chair was evolved, which continued well into the nineteenth century. The chair was made in two separate parts. The bottom part was a lowish table, wider at the front than the back, and had the brass fixture for a screw in the middle. The upper part was an armchair, with a cross stretcher like an X joining the four legs right at the bottom, and there was a brass screw fitment in the middle of the X. When a high-chair was needed the two sections were screwed together by a stout brass 'thumb screw'. The object of making the chair in this way was that it should serve at least two purposes: it would act as both a high- or low-chair, and when used as a low-chair there was a little table to go with it.

These chairs followed the fashion of the period from Chippendale to mid-Victorian times, and were invariably made of mahogany. Some really beautiful workmanship went into these chairs, which were sometimes little masterpieces but, to my mind, they have two great disadvantages. The first is that the screw fitting in the middle of the table means that nothing put down on it can lie really flat. The second is that when the screw is removed there is nowhere to put it until it is needed again. This is quite evident from the numbers of odd chairs and tables that have lost their partners. The chairs, as I have said, are often really beautiful, but marred by this X stretcher —people know at once what it has been. The stretcher can be taken away, but that leaves four tell-tale holes which, even when filled up, still give the game away. A chair that has once been part of something else, however lovely, is still not as valuable as one made separately.

The tables, once separated permanently from the chairs, are hardly any use at all; the brass screw fixture in the middle is both an eyesore and a nuisance. If it were not for this they could be used as low tea tables. I had one of these tables once that had had the top upholstered and turned into a stool. But as it had not been made to take the weight of an adult, one felt chary of using it. I have seen one country edition of this chair made in oak, but without the screw; both items were quite free-standing so to speak, and could easily have been sold separately without any difficulty. The table had a strong rim running round the edge, which held the chair quite tightly when in position. This was fine until the whole thing had to be moved. Then one forgot that the chair was not fixed to the base, and picked it up by the arms to move it, wondering why it was so light, not realising that the base was left exactly where it was, instead of coming with the chair.

TABLES

These are rare, though undoubtedly they were made in the seventeenth century in the form of small gate-legs, and in larger-than-usual joint stools. But when one comes to the eighteenth century they seem almost to disappear. I suppose it may have had something to do with the height of tables now being so much lower than the earlier tables were. A child from five onwards could sit on an ordinary chair to a gate-leg or drop-leaf table, but he could not so easily balance on a high-stool to a high refectory table.

Apart from these small, low gate-legs, I have seen only one table that had quite obviously been made for a child. It is pictured in Plate 29 with a child's 'comb-back' to go with it. Probably in the country the legs of a cricket table (page 32) were cut down to make it suitable for the use of a child. One does find quite a lot of low cricket tables, and this could be the reason.

BABY WALKERS

Baby walkers were simply made of a round ring of thick oak. This was hinged on one side and could be opened. When the baby had been put in, the ring was closed and fastened on the outside with a long iron latch. From this ring four legs curved widely outwards towards the bottom. As the bottom would come into contact with any object first, the baby would thus be saved from being knocked. Each leg was fitted with a castor. This was the usual country shape—of which there are some good examples in Snows Hill Museum, Broadway. An example I have seen of more elaborate cabinet-maker's work was an early eighteenth-century one of walnut, with six beautifully turned legs sloping outward, and inserted into a sexagonal stretcher at the bottom, into which the castors were fitted. A little tray was attached to the ring at the top to hold small toys or a rattle. These objects are very rare, and usually to be seen only in museums or private collections. There is a tiny one in a doll's house at the Bethnal Green Museum. Babies were not put into these walkers until they were on the verge of, or actually, walking.

BUREAUX AND DESKS

These, though one might not have suspected it, were country-made, as well as by the fashionable cabinet-maker. The workmanship was not skimped in any way just because they were made for children; the bureau illustrated in Plate 24 has even got secret drawers, and every succeeding owner must have loved it dearly. It is indeed a rare piece, that a child of five or six might have used, and though it was not every child who would have been scholarly enough to do so, it certainly attracted the delighted attention of every small boy or girl who saw it while it was in our care.

CRADLES

The shape of a cradle tells us whether it comes from a hot or cold country. Cradles from Italy and southern France are of

light design with no hoods, and quite shallow—no draughts
to be guarded against in these warmer climes! Those of the
colder countries are solid and deep and well-hooded. Even the
hoods can tell their own story, often being shaped, I am sure,
like the fashionable head-dresses of the time. There is the low,
squat Tudor shape, sometimes hinged to fold back when the
baby was taken out or put in, so as to avoid knocking the
child's head. Then there is the long sloping flat hood of the
Stuart period, cut away a bit in front; not so attractive this.
It can surely be no accident that the word 'hood' means a kind
of hat.

The earliest cradles of all were little four-post beds, with
the legs mounted on rockers, and hung all round with velvet
or brocade, with a tester of the same material. But this type
must have been found quite impracticable. There were no
sides to stop the baby from falling out, and the tester would
prevent anyone seeing at a quick glance what the child was
doing. Another early type was the barrel-shaped hooded
cradle, made by the cofferer of pine, and covered with brass-
studded velvet. This was not meant to go on the floor at all
but to stand on a coffer or table, or even on the mother's bed.

In Britain, until well into the eighteenth century, deep oak
cradles, carved, panelled or plain, with varying hoods and
unobtrusive rockers, were fashionable (Plate 32).

The cradles were deep, in order to accommodate the bed-
ding necessary in those days before the convenience of rubber
sheets and turkish towelling. According to early accounts, first
came a bed of rushes, then a straw mattress, then the sheet and
pillow. The damp rushes were replaced each day, and a dry
straw mattress was provided. Some cradles have the end panel
hinged, so that it opens like a door, in order to make the
necessary sweeping out easier. When the tightly swaddled
child was installed in the cradle, another sheet and blankets
would go on top, and the whole was then surrounded by a

K

'coverlid', ie coverlet, which was fastened by loops to the little knobs, often still found on the sides of the cradle.

The cradles were made with posts at each corner, which projected below the body, like short legs. These were cut up for about two inches and the top edges of the rockers inserted, and pegged in with wooden pegs. This made replacement easy when the rockers got worn down, or when legs were attached so that the cradle became a bed for an older child. The top ends of the two posts at the foot of the cradle extended a few inches upwards and were finished with knot-like finials. Two similar shaped finials were placed at the back of the hood. These four knobs were meant to facilitate the carrying of the cradle but, according to the illuminations in ancient manuscripts, they were also used for the mother to wind her wool on.

The rockers on early cradles do not project very far, and are very slightly curved so that only a gentle movement is caused by rocking. The rockers themselves have many interesting diversities. Some are beautifully shaped, and look most attractive viewed from either end. Unpanelled cradles did not have posts, and were much lower on the ground, because the rockers had to be screwed to the base of the cradle some three or four inches from each end. The mother needed to be seated on a low nursing-chair or stool in order to rock the cradle in comfort.

In humble homes the mother rocked the cradle, or else deputed one of the elder children to do so. Even father, according to Langland's 'Piers Plowman', was hauled out of bed in the middle of the night to perform this unwanted task. But in royal and noble households people were specially employed to keep the cradle rocking, the cradles so rocked being very often cots suspended between posts. Holes were made towards the top of the cot at each side through which straps or sashes were threaded and the cot was rocked by simply pulling on these. Persons so employed were called 'Rockers' and the job was considered an honour, and usually fell to the pages to perform. It is no uncommon thing to find an early oak cradle with crumbling floor-boards, due to rotting caused by damp stone floors—and damper babies. It is quite a legitimate repair to have the floors replaced.

Eighteenth-century cradles were somewhat smaller, not so squat in shape, and had rounded hoods. By this time chairs had ousted stools for common use, so the rockers, which were screwed to the base, were made much deeper to give height to the cradle and were much more rounded. The oak was much lighter in colour than the earlier oak; ash, elm, fruit-wood and pine were also used. Cradles made of pine were grained and varnished to imitate oak. We now find them 'stripped'. Occasionally one finds Scandinavian cradles of painted pine, the outsides gay with stylised flowers, the insides plain red or green. They are usually smaller than our cradles, but very decorative.

Cradles, as well as figuring in fairy tales and history, also figure in nursery rhymes. The best known lullaby both in Britain and America is 'Rock-a-bye Baby'. In America it is said that the words were composed by a young Pilgrim lad from the *Mayflower*, who was fascinated by the way the Red Indians hung their cradles of birch-bark in the branches of the trees. But it was not only Red Indians who did this, for it seems to have been a common practice long ago in Europe to put lightweight cradles, probably made of osiers, into trees for the wind to rock them while the mothers were at work, either in the fields, or washing clothes out of doors. Scotland has a version:

> I've placed my cradle on yond holly top
> And aye, as the wind blew, my baby did rock.

A Regency book, *Songs for the Nursery*, includes the well-known nursery rhyme beginning:

Hush a bye baby,
Thy cradle is green...

It *may* have been a green-painted cradle, but was much more likely to have been made of green osiers—a 'tree-cradle'.

BEDS

Apart from the truckle or trundle bed there were very few beds made specially for children; they slept with their sisters and brothers in full-sized four-poster beds. In the country mansions there may have been a specially made small four-poster for some pampered child; in the small cottages they were put in 'bed-cupboards' to sleep on hay or straw mattresses.

Truckle or Trundle Beds

This type was a very simple affair. A 'truckle' or 'trundle' was a wooden wheel, perhaps one might call it the equivalent of the modern castor, and these wheels were fixed to each corner of a shallow wooden box, made just big enough to take a straw mattress. The whole was 'truckled' or 'trundled' under the big four-poster bed in the day-time, and brought out at night for the children to sleep in. In very early days a man or woman's body servant slept on the truckle bed—hence the meaning of the verb 'to truckle', meaning to behave with servility to anyone. Probably in very cold weather the children slept in underneath the parents' bed, where the valances would act as curtains to keep out the draughts. At the present day one would probably find them only in museums.

Glossary

ASTRAGALS: Commonly the ornamental wooden moulding on glass doors.

CABRIOLE: The double curve on a furniture leg. The upper part swelling out, the lower swinging in towards the foot.

CANTED: Sides set at a slope, or legs of furniture with one side bevelled.

COCK BEADING: Small half-rounded projecting moulding applied to the edges of drawers.

CRESTING RAIL: The top rail of chairs, sometimes carved or decorated.

DROP HANDLES: Handles which hang, usually pear-shaped.

ESCUTCHEON: The fitting over a keyhole or back of a handle.

FIELDED: Panel joined by moulding, grooving or bevelling around a plain surface.

LOPERS: Sliding arms which support the lid of a desk or leaf of a table.

SPLAT: Flat central vertical member in a chair back.

STILES: Pieces of upright wood joining the framework of a piece of furniture.

STRETCHER: Cross pieces or rungs connecting legs of chairs, tables, etc.

TREEN: ie 'of trees'. Small pieces of wood-ware.

VOIDER: A name once applied to trays, but is really the name of any piece of furniture into which rubbish or waste is 'voided'.

Country Woods

Oak, walnut and mahogany are well known as woods. Other woods are not so well known, and below is given an alphabetical list of woods chiefly used in the making of country furniture.

Apple A hard wood, browny-pink in colour, which polishes well, and which was used for the making of small pieces of furniture.

Ash As ash 'burrs' are beautifully figured, and are capable of veneer matching, the wood was used for this purpose as well as for furniture making. The colour varies from a light honey-colour to a medium brown.

Beech A useful wood for the furniture maker as it is easier to work than oak, yet tough and difficult to split. It was much used for the 'hoops' of Windsor chairs. Light brown in colour.

Birch Much used to simulate other woods. Not so reliable as beech. The *bark* of the tree was used for snuff boxes made of 'pressed' wood. (Also as a groundwork for moose-hair embroidery in early Canada.)

Box Close-grained and heavy, very popular for small crisp carvings and inlays. In colour, an ivory-yellow to a warm brown.

167

Cedar There are many kinds of this wood. The English cedar and Italian cypress were both used for making chests and boxes of every description. It is an excellent wood for the preservation of clothes, for not only has it got a pleasant aromatic scent, but it is a moth repellent.

Cherry A hard fine-grained wood of a reddish-brown. Much used for country furniture as it does not warp.

Chestnut Not unlike oak in texture, grain and colour, but not so strong or hard wearing. It was used a great deal for floorboards and roof timbers as a substitute for oak when the latter wood was in demand for ship-building.

Elm As popular as oak in the country for the making of furniture—and also for the making of coffins. (As cabinet-makers were also undertakers, this is quite understandable.) A brownish colour with a handsome grain—but inclined to warp.

Laburnum A beautifully grained black and yellow wood used for inlaying, and the turning of small domestic pieces in the seventeenth and eighteenth centuries. Because of its colour it is often mistaken for lignum vitae, but it is not so heavy. Very rare to find furniture made of this wood.

Lignum vitae The hardest of all woods, and so heavy that it will sink in water. It is a mid-to-dark brown colour with lightish streaks, and was much used in the seventeenth century for drinking vessels such as wassail bowls and goblets. Being so hard it was also popular for pestles and mortars. In the early nineteenth century strong barrels were made of it. When it was introduced into Europe from the West Indies and Central America in the sixteenth century, it was considered to have a medicinal quality.

Lime Used for food moulds—and also for carving. Grinling

Gibbons did much fine work in this medium. It is a pale cream colour. The inner bark, when shredded, is used for gardener's 'bass'.

Mulberry   A hard, golden-brown wood, with dark streaks.

Pear   A hard, fine-grained pinkish wood with darker flecks. Very much used for carving. Many eighteenth-century picture-frames were made of this wood.

Pine   The commonest soft wood. Used for drawer-linings and the carcases of lacquered, veneered, and painted furniture. A pale cream colour that darkens with age to honey-colour.

Plum   A hard, heavy wood, being of a yellowish colour with a deep red heart. Used for country furniture.

Sycamore   Light in colour and very hard-wearing. As it can be scrubbed without raising the grain, almost all kitchen and dairy utensils were made of it. So were platters and roundels. Dyed to a greenish-grey this wood was used in the eighteenth century for fine veneering when it was called 'harewood'.

Yew   Hard, close-grained, red-brown wood, with a nearly white sapwood. It is resistant to decay, takes a high polish, was used for chairs and other small pieces of furniture. (And also in the seventeenth century for veneers.) With its natural knots, whorls, and wavy grain, it was a favourite choice for splats of Windsor chairs.

Dates of Period Furniture

Commonwealth Period	1649—1660	
Charles II: Restoration	1660—1685	17th Century
James II	1685—1689	(Oak and Walnut)
William and Mary	1689—1702	
William III		
Queen Anne	1702—1714	
George I	1714—1727	18th Century
George II	1727—1760	(Mahogany and Fruitwood)
George III	1760—1811	Early 19th Century
Regency	1811—1820	
George IV	1820—1830	19th Century
William IV	1830—1837	
Victoria	1837—1901	'Victoriana'

Books for Further Reading

Cescinsky and Webster. *English Domestic Clocks* (1968)
Wenham, Edward. *Old Clocks* (1963)

FURNITURE

Connoisseur Period Guides
Davies, Twiston and Johnson, Lloyd. *Welsh Furniture* (1950)
Jekyll, Gertrude and Jones, Sydney. *Old English Household Life* (1945)

PEWTER

Michaelis, R. F. *British Pewter* (1969)

QUILTING

Colby, Averil. *Quilting* (1972)

TREEN

Pinto, E. H. *Treen or Small Woodware* (1949)
Pinto, E. H. *Treen and Other Wooden Bygones* (1969)

Acknowledgements

My thanks are due to Mr Frith of Hills & Saunders, Eton, who took a great many of the photographs; to Ronnie Murray for her excellent line drawings; to the Librarians of the Eton branch of the Buckinghamshire County Library for their help in obtaining books; and last, but not least, to my husband, for listening so patiently to all I have written.

Index

Page numbers in italic indicate illustrations

(misnamed), 120-1
Windsor chairs, 38-45, *54*, *125*
Wine tables (misnamed), 31-2, *144*
Wool winders, 116-17, *125*
Work-tables, 34

Writing desks, 86-98, *106*; children's, 160; secret drawers in, 97-8

Yeoman tables, 26, *35*
Yew-tree chairs, 42, *125*